Dimensions of Helping Behaviour

INTERNATIONAL SERIES IN EXPERIMENTAL SOCIAL PSYCHOLOGY

Series Editor: Michael Argyle, University of Oxford

Vol 1. BOCHNER
Cultures in Contact

Vol 2. HOWITT
The Mass Media and Social Problems

Vol 3. PEARCE
The Social Psychology of Tourist Behaviour

Vol 4. COLMAN
Game Theory and Experimental Games

Vol 5. ALBERT
Genius and Eminence

Vol. 6 SMITHSON, AMATO and PEARCE
Dimensions of Helping Behaviour

A Related Pergamon Journal

LANGUAGE & COMMUNICATION*

An Interdisciplinary Journal

Editor: Roy Harris, *University of Oxford*

The primary aim of the journal is to fill the need for a publicational forum devoted to the discussion of topics and issues in communication which are of interdisciplinary significance. It will publish contributions from researchers in all fields relevant to the study of verbal and non-verbal communication.

Emphasis will be placed on the implications of current research for establishing common theoretical frameworks within which findings from different areas of study may be accommodated and interrelated.

By focusing attention on the many ways in which language is integrated with other forms of communicational activity and interactional behaviour it is intended to explore ways of developing a science of communication which is not restricted by existing disciplinary boundaries.

*Free specimen copy available on request.

NOTICE TO READERS

Dear Reader

An invitation to Publish in and Recommend the Placing of a Standing Order to Volumes Published in this Valuable Series.

If your library is not already a standing/continuation order customer to this series, may we recommend that you place a standing/continuation order to receive immediately upon publication all new volumes. Should you find that these volumes no longer serve your needs, your order can be cancelled at any time without notice.

The Editors and the Publisher will be glad to receive suggestions or outlines of suitable titles, reviews or symposia for editorial consideration: if found acceptable, rapid publication is guaranteed.

ROBERT MAXWELL
Publisher at Pergamon Press

Dimensions
of Helping Behaviour

by

MICHAEL SMITHSON
PAUL R. AMATO
&

PHILIP PEARCE
Behavioural Sciences Department, James Cook University

PERGAMON PRESS
OXFORD · NEW YORK · TORONTO · SYDNEY · PARIS · FRANKFURT

U.K.	Pergamon Press Ltd., Headington Hill Hall, Oxford OX3 0BW, England
U.S.A	Pergamon Press Inc., Maxwell House, Fairview Park, Elmsford, New York 10523, U.S.A.
CANADA	Pergamon Press Canada Ltd., Suite 104, 150 Consumers Road, Willowdale, Ontario M2J 1P9, Canada
AUSTRALIA	Pergamon Press (Aust.) Pty. Ltd., P.O. Box 544, Potts Point, N.S.W. 2011, Australia
FRANCE	Pergamon Press SARL, 24 rue des Ecoles, 75240 Paris, Cedex 05, France
FEDERAL REPUBLIC OF GERMANY	Pergamon Press GmbH, Hammerweg 6, D-6242 Kronberg-Taunus, Federal Republic of Germany

First edition 1983

Library of Congress Cataloging in Publication Data

Smithson, Michael.
Dimensions of helping behaviour
(International series in experimental social psychology)
Includes bibliographical references and indexes.
1. Helping behaviour. 2. Altruism. I. Amato, Paul R.
II. Pearce, Philip L. III. Title. IV. Series.
BF637.H4S63 1983 302'.14 82-14989

British Library Cataloguing in Publication Data

Smithson, Michael
Dimensions of helping behaviour.—(The International series in experimental social psychology; v. 6)
1. Social psychology
I. Title II. Amato, Paul R.
III. Pearce, Philip IV. Series
302 HM251
ISBN 0-08-027412-9

Printed in Great Britain by A. Wheaton & Co. Ltd., Exeter

Acknowledgements

THE authors wish to thank the nursing staff at the Townsville General Hospital, the students in the Behavioural Sciences Department at James Cook University, and the members of the Townsville community who generously participated in our research, and without whom the project would have been impossible. We would also like to thank Nerina and Marie Caltabiano, and Cathy Britton for their invaluable assistance in preparing initial drafts of the manuscript, and Dr. Wayne Bartz at the American River College for his generous offer of class time and students for our work. Finally, we acknowledge a debt of gratitude to the Special Research Grant Scheme at James Cook University for crucial financial support during several phases of the project.

Contents

Introduction to the Series

MICHAEL ARGYLE

SOCIAL psychology is in a very interesting period, and one of rapid development. It has survived a number of "crises", there is increased concern with external validity and relevance to the real world, the repertoire of research methods and statistical procedures has been greatly extended, and a number of exciting new ideas and approaches are being tried out.

The books in this series present some of these new developments; each volume contains a balance of new material and a critical review of the relevant literature. The new material consists of empirical research, procedures, theoretical formulations, or a combination of these. Authors have been asked to review and evaluate the often very extensive past literature, and to explain their new findings, methods or theories clearly.

The authors are from all over the world, and have been very carefully chosen, mainly on the basis of their previous published work, showing the importance and originality of their contribution, and their ability to present it clearly. Some of these books report a programme of research by one individual or a team, some are based on doctoral theses, others on conferences.

Social psychologists have moved into an increasing number of applied fields, and a growing number of practitioners have made use of our work. All the books in this series have been of some practical application, some will be on topics of wide popular interest, as well as adding to scientific knowledge. The books in the series are designed for advanced undergraduates, graduate students and relevant practitioners, and in some cases for a rather broader public.

We do not know how social psychology will develop, and it takes quite a variety of forms already. However, it is a great pleasure to be associated with books by some of those social psychologists who are developing the subject in such interesting ways.

1

Introduction and Plan of the Book

P. PEARCE, P.R. AMATO and M. SMITHSON

Social Psychological Research: Some Recent Concerns

THE DOMINANT tradition in social psychological research has been an experimental, laboratory-based mode of inquiry. Researchers using this approach attempt to understand important social behaviour through the control and manipulation of factors which influence simulated forms of the target behaviours. This research reflects a positivist philosophy of science and a limited deterministic view of human action.

For at least a decade now social psychologists have been systematically examining their discipline. The critical commentary has been variously labelled as a crisis in social psychology, a transition phase, an epistemological confrontation and a paradigm shift (Armistead, 1974; Harré and Secord, 1972; Strickland, Aboud and Gergen, 1976; Gilmour and Duck, 1980; Ginsburg, 1979). Some key criticisms of the experimental tradition have included the observation that the research is not cumulative. Specifically, this view suggests that it is difficult to link and integrate the plethora of individual studies which are published since (1) they use different independent and dependent variables, (2) have unique subject samples, (3) and they are replicated infrequently. A second criticism addresses the external validity of the social behaviour simulated in the laboratory. Just as ethologists have criticized experimental psychologists for studying a limited range of species divorced from their natural setting, so have social psychologists been attacked for a reliance on student populations, an atrophied range of behaviours, and above all a poor correspondence between the operationalized version of behaviour studied in the laboratory and its non-research referent. Thus, crowding is studied by observing students' responses in a high-density research room, helping by measuring the number of spilled computer cards a stranger will pick up for an experimenter, and love by the amount of eye contact between dating couples. The core argument here is not that social psychologists are interested in the wrong topics, but rather that the limited laboratory paradigm they employ trivializes many of the phenomena they attempt to study.

A third key criticism has been directed at the hidden assumptions about

2

the control of human action which accompany the traditional research approaches. Here it is argued that the response options for the subjects are frequently so constrained that experimenters fail to appreciate that there might be many alternative views of the experiment and a much wider range of responses than those selected for empirical study.

There have been other criticisms too. A concern has been expressed that social psychology is politically conservative, since it studies social behaviour from a self-contained individual or small group perspective (Sampson, 1978). According to Gergen (1978), a consequence of this political conservatism has been the impotence of the discipline when confronted with the problem of offering fresh alternatives to social problems.

A Short History of Helping Research

At the same time as these powerful criticisms of social psychology were being formulated the field of helping has been growing quite dramatically. This growth is illustrated in Figure 1.1.

Clearly helping has been a popular and expanding research area in the 1970s. This very popularity, set against the background of the previous problems in social psychology, raises several questions. For example, is helping as a topic of study less prone to these general criticisms or, indeed, has it found answers to them? Or is it the case that researchers concerned with helping have ignored many of the attacks on social psychology? Finally, is the proliferation of studies simply a reflection of the increasing pressures on the academic community to publish?

A close analysis of Figure 1.1 pinpoints the growth period in the helping area and in turn answers some of these questions. The study of helping can be conceived as beginning in the mid-1960s following increasing public concern over antisocial behaviour such as public assaults and murders and the frequently publicized absence of prosocial behaviours, e.g. in cases of bystander non-intervention (Rosenthal, 1964). Isolated surveys, public opinion polls and analysis of police records characterize the early research. The most marked rise in the number of studies according to both of the assessment procedures employed lies between 1970 and 1976. This period corresponds particularly with the publication and popularity of the work of Latané and Darley (1970) on bystander intervention. As Innes (1980) has argued, the phenomenon of eponymy, which may be defined as the association of specific individuals with the development and refinement of a concept in multiple publications, may greatly facilitate research development through a focusing of the field and the growth of author networks. The work of Latané and Darley has occupied just such a central role in the helping area. For example, in 1973 and 1974 their work was cited by 82

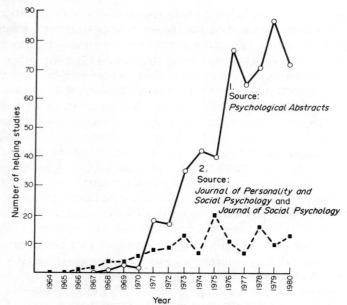

Fig. 1.1   Number of helping studies by year.

1. For the years 1964–1972 there were no entries under the heading of Assistance (Social Behaviour). Consequently the Interpersonal Processes heading was used and only those studies referring to helping were counted. The effect of this procedure was to limit the number of articles included under the rubric helping compared with the more explicit coverage obtained by individually reviewing articles in the two journals mentioned.

2. For 1964 the *Journal of Social and Abnormal Psychology* was used instead of the *Journal of Personality and Social Psychology* which commenced Volume 1 in 1965.

percent and 74 percent of the papers included in Figure 1.1 from the *Journal of Social Psychology* and the *Journal of Personality and Social Psychology*.

Other influences undoubtedly assisted the dramatic growth in the helping literature. The general growth of field studies in social psychology provided the right kind of research strategy and context for the non-laboratory helping work (cf. Bickman and Henchy, 1972). Extrinsic, non-intellectual factors also shaped the growth of helping studies. For example, many helping behaviours can be easily seen and measured, thus making research practical and inexpensive. It is likely too that contemporary social and cultural concerns in the United States (e.g. Vietnam and the peace movement) at the end of the 1960s may have created a *zeitgeist*, stimulating younger researchers to study prosocial, non-aggressive behaviour.

One can argue that the continued development and the currently high publication rates for helping studies support the view that the area has become an important and central topic in social psychology. Indeed, as will be argued presently, one of the immediate problems of helping research is that numerous theoretical perspectives derived from other areas of psychology and social psychology have been applied to the topic with each of these applications generating more studies and specific evidence relevant to the appropriate theory. For the present purposes it is sufficient to note that the research activity has been maintained at a high level for the last 8–10 years. The question at issue then becomes whether the helping field answers the social psychology critics who complain in general of (1) a lack of cumulative research, (2) low external validity, (3) a limited view of human action and (4) political and social conservatism.

Regrettably, a critical examination of the helping literature reveals that all of these criticisms have some potency, but perhaps the low external validity criticism has been the most satisfactorily answered in the helping area. As suggested before, the number of realistic field studies being conducted is quite high, although one should note that there is sometimes a trend towards using small inconsequential helping acts to represent large-scale phenomena such as human caring and empathy.

However, if the flight to the field, interspersed with a continuing tradition of some laboratory studies, may have partly answered the relevance critique, important problems concerning the non-cumulative nature of the research and a failure to provide a new non-deterministic model of human action still persist. The lack of socially innovative ideas stemming from the helping literature is also a fair criticism but perhaps somewhat premature since the area is of such recent origin and beset, as will be shown, with internal problems of understanding and development.

The non-cumulative nature of the research will be addressed here as the first major problem to be treated in this volume. It will be argued subsequently that the development of an alternative view of the individual's role in the helping situation may arise from an attempt to answer this first criticism. Quite simply, the problem may be stated as follows. Frequently, many small-scale helping studies are conducted which leave little impression and which are rarely cited in subsequent work because the measures used and populations studied prevent any realistic linking of the findings to other material. In addition, numerous areas of helping research bear little relationship to one another because the prevailing theoretical perspectives employed cast the studies into separate and highly specialized moulds. To understand the complexity and force of this criticism it is necessary to provide a review of a few of these areas in some detail. These theoretical pieces represent attempts to organize the field of helping. They are directly concerned, in their own way, with the non-cumulative nature of the field. It will be argued here, however, that these theoretical pieces are in fact a part of the problem they seek to rectify.

Theoretical Approaches to the Study of Helping

Explanations of helping can be divided into two basic types. On the one hand are those general theories of human behaviour which have been "borrowed" from the larger field of psychology. On the other hand are those medium-range theories with a specific orientation which have been developed exclusively within the helping literature.

Social psychologists working in the first category begin by taking a theory which has explanatory power in some other area of psychology or social science and use it to explain some aspect of helping. Examples of these "borrowed" theories include social learning theory (Bandura, 1971; Rosenhan, 1978; Rushton, 1980), equity theory (Walster, Walster and Berscheid, 1978; Hatfield, Walster and Piliavin, 1978), attribution theory (Ickes and Kidd, 1976; Weiner, 1980), cognitive developmental theory (Kohlberg, 1969, 1976; Krebs, 1978), Lewinian-based promotive-tension theory (Hornstein, 1972, 1978), reactance theory (Brehm, 1966; Goodstadt, 1971) and social comparison theory (Festinger, 1954; Smith, Vanderbilt and Callen, 1973). Typically, deductions are made about two or more situations in which the theory predicts differential rates of helping. Research is then conducted to test the theoretical predictions.

To illustrate such approaches, five general theories of behaviour and their application to various aspects of helping will be discussed. These are social learning theory, cognitive developmental theory, equity theory, sociobiological theory, and attribution theory. While this cannot be a comprehensive review, the main trend of this level of theorizing may be understood by these examples.

Secondly, a few middle-range approaches and theories which have been developed specifically within the helping literature will be considered. Examples of theories with a specific helping orientation include Latané and Darley's decision-making model of bystander intervention (1970), Schwartz's theory of personal helping norms (1977), theories based upon the concept of empathy (Aronfreed, 1968; Rosenhan, 1970; Hornstein, 1978) and the body of work dealing with the effect of temporary mood states on helping (Isen and Levin, 1972; Baumann, Cialdini and Kenrick, 1981).

Following the outline of these approaches to helping, a reconsideration of the role of theory in this area will be undertaken, with specific reference to the problem of non-cumulative research.

The Social Learning Approach

The social learning approach interprets helping as a form of behaviour learned from other people. As such, social learning theorists emphasize the established learning principles of reinforcement, observation and modelling in understanding and explaining prosocial behaviour. Helping could be learned, for example, through a process of operant conditioning in which a child is rewarded for behaving in a prosocial manner or is punished for behaving in an antisocial manner. More importantly, helping responses can be learned vicariously, through the observation of other people behaving prosocially in certain situations and the positive consequences which result from it.

This approach has generated a large number of empirical studies, many using children as subjects. For example, studies done with children have shown that the amount of sharing behaviour exhibited can be increased if rewards are made contingent upon its occurrence (e.g. Fischer, 1963: Midlarsky, Bryan and Brickman, 1973).

The lion's share of studies, however, have dealt with the effects of observation and modelling. Research by Bryan (1972), Bryan and Walbeck (1970), Grusec (1971), Rosenhan and White (1967), Rushton (1973), and others have demonstrated that if children see another person behaving generously, they will behave more generously themselves. If they see another person modelling selfish behaviour, however, they may behave less generously. Furthermore, research has shown that these modelling effects tend to persist in time and can generalize to somewhat different situations. Similar modelling effects have also been demonstrated in adults as well. In one study Bryan and Test (1967) used two field situations: a person with a broken-down car along the highway and a person soliciting donations for charity. They found that the presence of a helping model significantly increased the helping rate for passers-by in both situations.

In many of these studies there were no extrinsic rewards or reinforcers present. Thus, explanations for the powerful effects of modelling have focused more upon the notion that through observation of a helping model, the individual acquires standards for his own behaviour. Meeting, or failing to meet, these acquired standards can then result in self-reward or self-punishment (Rosenhan, 1978). In this way, prosocial forms of behaviour can become self-reinforcing, and hence, stable components of a person's behavioural repertoire. However, the generality of these acquired standards is often not clear, for a person who learns to exhibit one particular form of helping behaviour, like donating, will not necessarily exhibit a somewhat different form of helping, like rescuing (Weissbrod, 1976). The extent of generalization from one helping form to the next remains problematic.

The Cognitive Development Approach

Like social learning theory, the cognitive developmental approach is also concerned with how individuals learn appropriate forms of behaviour, but instead of focusing upon external environmental contingencies, the cognitive developmental approach emphasizes the individual's progress through ordered stages of cognitive structure. These structures represent ways of thinking about and making sense out of the world, and are hierarchical, with later stages reflecting more advanced forms of thinking. An individual's ability to reason morally and engage in prosocial behaviour is seen as being dependent upon his overall level of cognitive maturation (see Krebs, 1978 for a discussion of this approach).

Piaget (1932) held that there are two levels of moral reasoning. The first, heteronomous morality, is characterized by the evaluation of right and wrong on the basis of an action's consequences. The second, autonomous morality, is characterized by an emphasis on the actor's intentions, rather than the consequences of the action. Lawrence Kohlberg (1969, 1976) expanded upon Piaget's model and proposed six stages of moral development. According to Kohlberg, growth from a lower to a higher stage is dependent upon the individual's increased intellectual ability, a decline in egocentrism, and an increased ability to take the role of the other. For example, at a stage 1 level of moral reasoning, people may engage in prosocial behaviour because it results in concrete rewards and the avoidance of punishments. By the time the person has progressed to stage 4 thinking, the notion of abstract rules has been internalized. People at this stage may engage in prosocial behaviour and avoid antisocial behaviour, not so much because of the concrete rewards and punishments involved, but because authority deems that it should be so. Those individuals who reach the highest stage of moral development are motivated by internalized abstract values which may, at times, come into conflict with the laws of society. Thus a person using stage 6 reasoning might argue that it is ethically correct to steal if it results in saving the life of a starving person, a higher good which transcends the law.

While social learning theorists have concerned themselves mainly with the environmental contingencies which lead to the occurrence of prosocial acts (such as the presence of a model), researchers in the cognitive development tradition have been mainly concerned with the moral rules which people use in thinking about behaving prosocially. They argue that individuals will exhibit different patterns of prosocial behaviour depending upon how they interpret situations within the context of their understanding of morality. Cognitive developmental researchers thus argue that a given act of helping can only be interpreted in the light of what the act means to the individual and how that act fits into larger cognitive structures

(Krebs, 1978). Thus, most researchers in this tradition have not concerned themselves as much as other researchers with the actual occurrence, or non-occurrence, of prosocial behaviours in experimental settings. Instead, the individual's level of moral reasoning, as inferred from verbal responses to hypothetical situations, is used as the main dependent variable which is then related to background variables such as age, social class and culture, or manipulated variables such as exposure to moral dilemmas.

Krebs (1978) argues that the quantity of helping does not necessarily increase with higher stages of development. However, qualitatively speaking, the individual's reasons for engaging in prosocial behaviour will change markedly, and increasing maturity will mean that behaviour will become less egocentric and more in tune with the needs of others. Nevertheless, in spite of Kreb's assertion that higher levels of moral reasoning should not be correlated with higher rates of helping, a number of studies have found just such relationships (Emler and Rushton, 1974; Harris, Mussen and Rutherford, 1976; Rubin and Schneider, 1973; Staub, 1974).

Equity Theory

Equity theory focuses upon one important set of social norms relevant to the understanding of patterns of prosocial behaviour: norms of equity. It begins by postulating that societies evolve norms such that individuals engaged in social transactions should receive equal rewards, proportional to their costs. In this way, the overall distribution of rewards and costs for members of a collectivity is maximized. Within this normative system, individuals who perceive relationships they are in to be inequitable will experience distress. People in such situations will attempt to correct the imbalance by creating more equitable conditions. This can be done behaviourally, as when an exploiter compensates his victim or when a victim seeks restitution for exploitation. It can also occur psychologically with an individual restoring equity by rationalizing his role of exploiter or victim. Just how an individual decides to restore equity depends upon the various rewards and costs associated with each strategy. Generally, individuals will utilize strategies which minimize their costs and maximize their outcomes within the constraints of the normative system (see Walster, Walster and Berscheid, 1978 for a discussion of this approach).

Equity theory makes a number of predictions about helping behaviour. For example, it predicts that the more responsibility a person feels for the suffering of a victim, the more likely she or he will be to make restitution to the victim. Avoidance of the victim, however, might be the result if it is more costly to restore equity than it is to abandon the relationship. In responding to an emergency, for example, potential interveners will have to weigh the rewards for intervening (thanks, praise, perceived competence, monetary rewards, etc.) against the possible costs (physical danger, amount of effort involved, embarrassment, etc.) (Hatfield, Walster and Piliavin, 1978).

This framework was used by Hatfield, Walster and Piliavin (1978) to account for the findings of a field study (Piliavin and Piliavin, 1972) which examined the effect of blood on a victim's chances of being helped. It was found that the bleeding victim was helped less often than the non-bleeding victim, suggesting that the arousal and disgust at the sight of blood made it more difficult for bystanders to intervene. It was argued that it was less costly for bystanders in this situation to avoid the victim than to try to reduce the "inequity" of the situation by helping. A larger body of research, however, has explored the implications of norms of equity in more commonly occurring situations. For example, Lerner (1974) found that children who were overpaid for a job later donated more money to charity than children who were underpaid. A number of studies (e.g. Cialdini, Darby and Vincent, 1973; Freedman, Wallington and Bless, 1967) have shown that people who either cause harm to others or witness harm being done are motivated to compensate the victim in some way. Other studies by Gergen, Ellsworth, Maslach and Seipel (1975) and Gross and Latané (1974) indicate that people have a strong desire to reciprocate, on an equal basis, help which they have received. Finally, Schopler and Thompson (1968) found that help is less likely to be reciprocated if it is seen as selfishly motivated.

The Sociobiological Approach

The sociobiological approach attempts to explain human social behaviour, along with animal behaviour, in genetic and evolutionary terms. However, an explanation for altruistic behaviour in these terms appears to present a paradox, for altruism requires a degree of self-sacrifice. This being true, individual members of a species engaging in altruistic forms of behaviour would be expected to produce fewer offspring. Hence, their chances of carrying forward any genetically based altruistic tendencies into the next generation would be lower. Since differential rates of reproduction generate evolutionary change, it would be expected that the least altruistic members of a species would be the ones contributing the most genetic material to future generations. How, then, can the idea of a "gene" for altruism be reconciled with evolutionary notions of natural selection?

It is to this question that sociobiologists have devoted considerable attention. Three mechanisms have been postulated to account for the evolution of altruism. The first, group selection, assumes that entire populations of a species may possess different genotypes and may be in competition with each other. Individuals in a group with a strong predisposition toward altruistic self-sacrifice might indeed be more likely to perish. However, their self-sacrificing behaviour would increase the chances of survival for the other members of the group. By the same token, less altruistic groups, because of the lower frequency of altruistic behaviour among their members, would be less likely to survive. Since the beneficiaries carry the same altruistic genes, these genes would increase in the population as a whole. A theory based upon the notion of group selection was put forward by Wynne-Edwards (1962) to explain why some animals refrain from breeding when population densities become too large. However, most biologists believe that selection at the group level is too problematic to be important in the evolution of altruism (Wilson, 1975).

A second mechanism refers to kin selection (Wilson, 1975). In this process, the self-sacrificing behaviour of an individual increases the likelihood of survival (and hence, reproduction) of others who share identical genes by common descent. The concept of kin selection was first put forward by Charles Darwin to explain the behaviour of insect castes. A modern version of this idea was developed by Hamilton (1972) who proposed the concept of inclusive fitness. This concept refers to the sum of an individual's own fitness plus the fitness of all its relatives. According to this view, if an individual sacrifices its life for its family, it still ensures the continuation of identical genes into the next generation (for example, brothers and sisters share 50 percent of their genes in common). This perspective suggests that the more genes are shared by individuals, the more likely those individuals will be to engage in altruistic behaviour toward each other.

A third mechanism is that of reciprocal altruism, a concept introduced by Trivers (1971). According to Trivers, reciprocal altruism occurs when an altruistic individual is likely to be "paid back" by the recipient at a later date. Patterns of reciprocal altruism, while under genetic control, could still occur among individuals not related by common descent. Because reciprocal altruism requires enduring relationships and reliable memory, it is common in human society but is rare in animal societies.

While sociobiology is an increasingly popular approach (as evidenced by its inclusion in two recent volumes on helping: Wispé, 1978, and Rushton, 1980), its relevance to the social psychology of helping is still very slight in that it has generated little empirical research. However, some propositions from sociobiology are consistent with current knowledge about helping. For example, sociological research has shown that kin groups are regularly called upon, even in contemporary urban societies, for assistance. Bell and Boat (1957) found in the United States that the closer the kin, the greater the degree of mutual aid. Adams (1967) found that feelings of obligation to kin were still very strong among urbanites. Furthermore, feelings of obligation were stronger for kin than for friends. Bott (1971) in a study of London families found that both neighbours and kin were called upon in times of need, but the majority of emotional and material support was provided by family. Litwak and Szelenyi (1969) have argued that while friends and neighbours tend to be relied upon for many kinds of day-to-day assistance, kin are generally relied upon for more serious, long-term forms of helping. Thus, the prediction from sociobiology that helping behaviour should increase with relatedness (from strangers to friends to kin) is supported by the data.

However, it should be emphasized that a large number of psychologists, sociologists and other social scientists have been critical of the sociobiological approach. They have argued that sociobiologists have ignored the powerful effects of social learning and the extent to which altruistic behaviour can vary from culture to culture. Many social scientists prefer to think of altruism as a product of cultural evolution (for a discussion, see Cohen, 1978, and Campbell, 1978).

Attribution Theory

Attribution theory is concerned with the attributions people make about the causes of their own and other people's behaviour. While the foundations of the theory were laid by Heider (1958) it was later extended and developed by Rosenbaum (1972) and Weiner (1974). Out of this work grew a "taxonomy of causes" in which the basic underlying dimensions of perceived causality were identified. In a recent formulation, Weiner (1980) suggested that there are three fundamental dimensions which need to be understood in attribution theory. These are locus of control (internal versus external), stability (stable versus unstable) and controllability (controllable versus uncontrollable). The type of attribution which a person makes about the cause of another's behaviour is held to strongly influence both the attributor's affective reaction and his subsequent behaviour toward the target person. While Weiner's work was originally concerned with achievement motivation, both he and other attribution theorists have recently turned toward helping behaviour as a field to which attribution theory might contribute some explanatory principles (see Ickes and Kidd, 1976 for a general discussion of attribution theory and helping).

Ickes and Kidd (1976) postulate that if the cause of a victim's dependency is attributed to factors which are not intentional, that is, to factors over which the victim has no control, the observer will feel some responsibility to lend assistance to the victim. However, if the cause of a victim's dependency is attributed to something which is intentional, that is, to something which the victim can control, the observer will feel little compulsion to lend assistance. Thus, attribution theory predicts that more help will be given when dependency is due to, say, a lack of ability on the victim's part (internal but uncontrollable) than when it is due to a lack of effort on the victim's part (internal and controllable). Furthermore, Ickes and Kidd postulate that greater responsiveness to a request for help may occur when the observer attributes his own positive outcomes to his own ability rather than to his effort. Attributing success to ability (a stable attribute) may lead to feelings of competence and heightened self-esteem, a lowered perceived cost of helping (since positive outcomes can easily be reachieved) and an increased belief that helping will be successful, all making help-giving more likely.

Weiner's approach (1980) strongly emphasizes the mediating role of affect between attribution and helping. According to Weiner, perception of a person in need gives rise to a search for causation on the observer's part. If the observer attributes the cause of the other person's distress to internal, controllable factors, she or he is likely to feel anger and disgust. If, however, the observer attributes the cause to factors which are external and uncontrollable, feelings of sympathy and concern are likely to be generated. Because of the affect generated in the former situation, help is unlikely to be given, while in the latter situation the positive affect makes help-giving much more likely.

General support has been given to the attribution model of helping by a number of empirical studies. These include Ickes, Kidd and Berkowitz (1976), Barnes, Ickes and Kidd (1979), Meyer and Mulherin (1980) and Weiner (1980).

Other Approaches to the Study of Helping: The Search for Predictor Variables

The majority of helping studies have been guided by lower-level theories or approaches which lack the grand sweep of theories such as social learning theory or attribution theory. Operating in the absence of a broad theoretical framework, researchers have invested considerable effort in locating those variables which predict helping in a variety of settings.

Broadly, the empirical work can be divided into two blocks: those studies searching for stable personal characteristics of individuals relevant to helping, and those studies searching for situational variables relevant to helping. Each will be briefly discussed.

Personal Correlates of Helping

Studies in this area have considered both demographic characteristics of individuals such as age (Green and Schneider, 1974), social class (DePalma, 1974), sex and race (Wispé and Freshley, 1971) and urban versus rural background (Weiner, 1976); and stable, intrapsychic constructs such as personal norms (Schwartz, 1977), empathy (Aronfreed, 1970), self-concept (Trimakas and Nicolay, 1974), values (Staub, 1974), belief in a just world (Lerner, 1975), self-concern (Liebhart, 1972), ideological affiliation (Ehlert, Ehlert and Merrens, 1973), political orientation (Gaertner, 1973), self-labelling (Kraut, 1973), self-esteem (Rudestam, Richards and Garrison, 1971) and locus of control (Lerner and Reavy, 1975). Two of the most appealing clusters of studies, with both theoretical development and empirical support, revolve around the concepts of personal norms and empathy. Each of these will be discussed in turn.

According to Schwartz (1977), personal helping norms are internalized self-expectations of behaviour. These personal norms can be activated by the perception of another's need. Because the individual is motivated to act in ways consistent with his own values and sense of self-worth, the individual has a feeling of moral obligation to help. The strength of the obligation to help is affected by the strength and stability of the norms themselves, and certain characteristics of the person, such as his awareness of the consequences of his behaviour for others and his tendency to deny responsibility for acting. Schwartz (1977) uses these basic ideas to develop a complex decision-making theory of altruistic behaviour. Aspects of his theory have been supported by empirical studies (Schwartz, 1970, 1973, 1974, 1977; Schwartz and Ben David, 1976). Other studies concerned with norms include the work of Berkowitz and his associates dealing with the social responsibility norm (Berkowitz and Daniels, 1963, 1964), work done explicating the norm of reciprocity (e.g. Gouldner, 1960; Gergen, Ellsworth, Maslach and Seipel, 1975), and those studies done in the area of equity theory (discussed earlier).

Empathy is an alternative intrapsychic explanation for helping. Empathy refers to a person's ability to vicariously experience the emotions felt by others. The basic notion here is that individuals who share the distress of others will be motivated to help them. Theories of altruism based upon empathy have been developed by Aronfreed (1970) and Hornstein (1972, 1978). The importance of empathic responses in helping behaviour has been supported by a number of studies (Coke, Batson and McDavis, 1978; Liebhart, 1972; Krebs, 1975; Mehrabian and Epstein, 1972).

Situational Correlates of Helping

The work of Latané and Darley (1968, 1970) was in many ways pivotal in turning the attention of researchers toward situational variables relevant to helping. Their research in bystander intervention in emergencies revealed that the presence of other bystanders at the scene of an emergency could strongly decrease the likelihood of any single bystander intervening. They attributed this effect to two causes: diffusion of responsibility and the definition of the situation. They reasoned that in an emergency the amount of personal responsibility to help experienced by individuals tends to get diffused among other potential helpers present, the result often being that no one helps at all. Alternatively, a situation can develop in which no one wants to be the first person to act. Seeing that no one else is reacting can lead each person to define the situation as a non-emergency in which intervention is not required. In this way, the presence of others can lead to a state of "pluralistic ignorance". Latané and Darley incorporated their findings into a decision-making model of intervention. According to this model, an individual must first notice that something unusual is going on, define it as an emergency, accept personal responsibility for acting, and then decide what form of help to give, before he will actually intevene. At any step in the process, the "wrong" decision will mean the intervention does not occur.

The work of Latané and Darley raised serious doubts about the relevance of both social norms and personality characteristics as explanations for helping. Social norms, they argued, were too general and vague to account for behaviour in specific situations. Furthermore, they found that personality characteristics such as Machiavellianism and alienation did not predict whether a person would help or not. Generally, their work seemed to lead to the conclusion that stable, intrapsychic variables were not the most important ones for understanding overt helping behaviour. The power of the situation to affect behaviour was held to be so strong that it could override people's values, norms and personality dispositions.

Many researchers followed this idea and began investigating other situational determinants of helping in both emergency and everyday situations. The general strategy became one of identifying the salient characteristics of situations which encourage or inhibit helping responses. A list of the situational variables investigated would include the ambiguity of the situation (Clark and Word, 1974), the perceived competence of other bystanders (Bickman, 1971), the amount of cost involved in helping (Piliavin and Piliavin, 1972), the severity of the victim's distress (Shotland and Huston, 1979), the degree of dependency of the victim (Harris and Meyer, 1973), the style of request for help (Langer and Abelson, 1972), the degree of threat in the situation (Harris and Meyer, 1973), the physical attractiveness of the victim (Mims, Hartnett and Nay, 1975), the race of the recipient (Gaertner and Bickman, 1971), the language and dress of the recipient (Harris and Baudin, 1973), the amount of noise in the setting (Mathews and Canon, 1975), residential density (Bickman *et al.*, 1973), the degree of stimulus overload in the environment (Sherrod and Downs, 1974), the pleasantness of the environment (Amato, 1981b, 1981c), the familiarity of the recipient (Pearce, 1980) and ambient temperature

(Schneider, Lesko and Garrett, 1980).

One of the most appealing clusters of studies has been concerned with the influence of temporary affect states of the potential helper on helping behaviour. Affect is generally regarded in this line of research as a mediating variable between external situational variables and prosocial behaviour (Lau and Blake, 1976). Studies by Isen and Levin (1972), Rosenhan, Underwood and Moore (1974) and many others have demonstrated that a positive affect state leads to increased helping behaviour. The effect of a negative mood state, however, is less clear. Cialdini and his associates (Cialdini, Darby and Vincent, 1973) have argued that negative affect (such as sadness) leads to increased helpfulness as well. According to this view, altruistic behaviour is rewarding to the helper. Through socialization, the individual learns that behaving prosocially is self-gratifying. The self-imposed rewards associated with altruism then become motivators for later forms of helping. Therefore, helping behaviour is one possible strategy an individual can use to alleviate a negative affect state. Support for this view of altruism as "hedonism" comes from a number of studies (Cialdini, Darby and Vincent, 1973; Cialdini and Kenrick, 1976; Baumann, Cialdini and Kenrick, 1981).

In summary, it is not argued there that stable intrapsychic variables have been ignored by researchers: the earlier sections demonstrate that this was not the case. Nevertheless, it is probably true to say that the search for and manipulation of situational variables has been the most frequent research strategy in the helping studies of the seventies.

An Alternative Strategy for Theory Formulation

The preceding review of theoretical approaches to helping reveal several weaknesses in the current activity on this topic. First, it is apparent that each theory examines very different aspects of helping. For example, social learning theory investigates how the individual learns appropriate helping behaviour and helping norms, cognitive development theory examines the moral rules individuals use in thinking about prosocial acts, equity theory studies the ways in which helping behaviour is used to maintain equity, while attribution theory evaluates the inferences people make about the causes of the victim's distress and the effect this has upon the likelihood of help being given. The other approaches discussed have other similarly specific concerns within the helping area. As a consequence of the different interest areas of the theories, the studies generated in one framework are often irrelevant or uninterpretable in terms of the other perspectives. This lack of congruence among the research findings may be considered to be the second weakness in the current research activity. A third weakness may be defined as the spurious advancement in the field. As each theory develops its own supporting data base, there is an impression that each theoretical approach is advancing our knowledge and understanding of helping. But this apparent development is misleading because the limit or perimeter of generalizability of these research pieces remains unknown.

One remedy for many of these problems is to provide an overview of the helping research using a taxonomic, organizational approach to theory construction. Such an approach is akin to botanical classification in that it attempts to provide a descriptive account of the available material which will provide an organized basis for later, more refined research (Sokal and Sneath, 1963; Hartigan, 1975). This kind of approach to helping can be usefully related to the advocacy of pre-theoretical approaches in social psychology generally (McGuire, 1980; Forgas, 1980) and of a helping taxonomy in particular (Wispé, 1972; Staub, 1979).

On a general level McGuire has argued that a guiding idea or systems theory should precede empirical work and direct the observations. McGuire claims that the philosophical (1980:77) shadow of logical empiricism has haunted psychology researchers for too long and has forced them into an elaborate deceit when reporting research. According to this view, researchers spend much time thinking about their hypotheses, the situations in which they anticipate positive and negative results, and the experimental manipulations which are most likely to further their research aims. Such material is carefully expunged from the final research report. Instead of this approach which McGuire contends is the product of overly zealous adherence to the hypothetico-deductive rules of logical empiricism, a Constructivist paradigm for research is advanced. This position suggests that researchers conduct and publish systematic investigations which clarify the meaning of opposite hypotheses and indicate as clearly as possible the anticipated boundaries and generalities of their formulations. In McGuire's words: "According to the Constructivist paradigm the role of the empirical side of science is not to test which of the opposite formulations is valid but rather to explore and discover the range of circumstances in which each of the opposite formulations hold" (McGuire, 1980:79).

McGuire's advocacy of a pre-theoretical organization and honesty is echoed by Forgas (1980) who argues for a greater descriptive phase in research. Forgas claims that the hypothesis-testing phase has been considered more important than the critical hypothesis-generating phase of research. As a consequence, he suggests that theoretical models in many areas of social psychology have concentrated on narrow, unrepresentative and specific cases or phenomena. This has diverted many researchers into intellectual blind-alleys such as the topic of risky shift.

An example of the kind of organizational overview of a research topic which Forgas and McGuire advocate can be seen in the study by Falbo

(1977). Using a multidimensional scaling analysis Falbo examined power strategies that people use to get their own way. The explicit aim of the article was to derive a more inclusive conceptualization of power strategies and to discover the relationships which obtain amongst these strategies. It was demonstrated that two dimensions, rationality and directness, characterized the strategies people use, with the directness strategy being considered socially less desirable. Such a framework, it can be argued, can be used in future studies for theoretical purposes and for the selection of strategies for experimental manipulation.

Within the helping area itself the need for a taxonomy of helping situations or types has also been considered. Wispé drew attention to the need to develop a taxonomy of prosocial behaviours when he stated, "The different manifestations of positive social behaviours should be distinguished so that they can be operationalized more precisely and their genotypic similarities and differences noted" (Wispé, 1972:4). He then went on to distinguish and define six categories of prosocial behaviour: altruism, sympathy, co-operation, helping, aid and donating. These categories, however, are basically *a priori* creations, and how they might relate to one another remains largely unspecified.

Similarly, Lau and Blake talked about the "major forms of helping behaviour: donation of one's own resources to individuals or organizations, sharing of one's own resources with others, offering help to the needy, and crisis intervention" (Lau and Blake, 1976:2). However, this typology, like that of Wispé, does not appear to have been either empirically or theoretically derived, and is instead based upon a common-sense and somewhat arbitrary categorization.

Gottlieb (1978) argued for the development of a classificatory scheme of helping behaviours, and attempted to derive such a scheme from an empirical analysis of everyday helping activities as described in interview protocols. While this can be seen as a useful step, his 26 category scheme was specific to a narrow population (single, economically disadvantaged mothers) and was limited to the kinds of assistance they received from others. Because of its specificity, this scheme is not likely to be useful for the kind of general organizing function being argued for here.

In his major review of helping Staub (1979) reached similar conclusions about the need for a taxonomic organization. He argued that an understanding of helping would be facilitated by using the construct of "prosocial goal". Staub suggested that to make accurate predictions in the field of helping, the relative importance of the individual's goals must be understood in conjunction with the activitating potential of situations to elicit the prosocial goals. For Staub's model of helping it therefore becomes important to understand situations. Following Frederiksen (1972) and Mischel (1976), Staub argues that a systematic way of conceptualizing situations is required. Such a framework would then permit researchers to specify dimensions of situations that relate to certain goals and to conduct studies in which these situational properties are systematically varied along these dimensions.

Overall, several writers have argued that a pre-theoretical organizing framework for helping is needed. This taxonomy or systematic classification should be able to relate helping situations of different types to one another, it should enable researchers to vary the properties of situations along chosen dimensions, and it should guide researchers in their hypothesis testing and theory formulation. A taxonomy with these characteristics would allow separate research findings to be meaningfully compared, would help to establish the limits of empirical and theoretical generalizations, and would aid in the planning of future studies.

The organizing framework devised by the writers to fulfil these criteria will be presented in Chapter 2 of this volume. Subsequent chapters will refine and develop this framework. More detailed plans for the organization of this book are outlined below. As with all volumes of this nature it is hoped that most readers will wish to read through all of the chapters in the order in which they appear. However, readers with a particular interest in the taxonomy itself and its behavioural application may wish to concentrate more on Chapters 2, 3, 6 and 7 while those with more cognitive and methodological interests should find Chapters 2, 3, 4 and 5 of central concern.

Plan of the Book

The first and present chapter of this volume has attempted to identify some key criticisms of social psychology. Subsequently the development of the field of helping was examined and it was particularly noted that the published research showed a dramatic rise in the early 1970s, remaining an active field of inquiry into the 1980s. Nevertheless, many of the general problems of social psychology research also exist in the helping area, notably difficulties with non-cumulative research, an overly deterministic model of man and a certain political conservatism. The major theoretical approaches in helping research were briefly reviewed to document these problems and difficulties. From this review it was argued that a taxonomic organizational overview of the helping area is needed. This call for an organizing framework was shown to have important links with recent thinking in social psychological theory and the helping literature itself.

In Chapter 2 of this volume the basic strategy used in developing a taxonomy of helping is outlined. This approach is a cognitive one based upon people's perceptions of helping episodes. Multidimensional scaling procedures are used in a preliminary study to analyse similarity judgements given by subjects to a sample of helping episodes derived from the social psychological literature. Data analysis yields a stable, three-dimensional helping model with dimensions that are both meaningful and interpretable through regression procedures.

Chapter 3 extends the taxonomic approach of Chapter 2 into neglected areas of helping. It is proposed that the social psychological study of helping has ignored some important kinds of help. To substantiate this claim, a comprehensive lexicon of English terms which refer to helping is constructed, and gaps in the literature are located by having subjects point out those terms for which none of the studies in the sample from Chapter 2 are good examples. New episodes are then constructed which exemplify the missing terms, and these are rated by subjects for their similarity to the episodes in the old sample. The combined similarity ratings are submitted to a multidimensional scaling analysis similar to that performed in Chapter 2. The results indicate that there is a coherent region of helping in the space which has been neglected by social psychological researchers. The nature of this new region is investigated, and the entire space is used to provide a taxonomic organization of helping based on a representative sample of helping episodes.

Because the studies in Chapters 2 and 3 are based on university student samples, the question of generalizability needs to be addressed. Chapter 4 presents the results of replication studies involving five samples, with subjects from both university and non-university populations, one sample comprising American (rather than Australian) students. Multidimensional scaling analyses for individual samples and an individual differences scaling (INDSCAL) analysis for the combined data-set are employed to assess the stability and generalizability of the taxonomy presented in Chapter 3. While the major features of the taxonomy and its organizing dimensions appear stable and generalizable, some evidence points to the likely existence of important intergroup differences and even the possibility of an additional generalizable dimension. The helping literature has suggested that men and women may respond differently to some helping situations, and so the data are split by gender to explore sex differences. Additionally, differences between age-groups and political affiliations are explored.

Chapter 5 explores further topics in cognitions about helping. In the first section, data from the Chapter 3 study are used to illustrate methods for representing lexical categories of helping as graded contours in multi-dimensional space. These regional representations may be used to indicate which areas of the space are referenced by specific natural language categories. Applications for such representations include questionnaire and attitude-scale construction, as well as the tailored construction of helping episodes for empirical studies. The second section of the chapter illustrates the use of fuzzy-set methods for extending the capacity of the taxonomy to represent cognitive schema. An empirically based typology of natural language helping terms is generated which corresponds to the subjects' cognitive schema. This typology is then used to locate and interpret salient regions and clusters in the multidimensional space.

In Chapter 6 the helping taxonomy developed in previous chapters is applied to the study of behaviour. This chapter begins by addressing a few general issues in relating cognitions about helping to prosocial behaviour and argues that the implicit schema people use to make judgements about helping episodes are relevant to understanding everyday helping in non-laboratory contexts. The results of three empirical studies are then presented. The first study is a large-scale field experiment comparing rates of prosocial behaviour in urban and rural settings in Australia. In this study, six measures of helping are used, the choice of measures having been guided by the taxonomy. The taxonomy is then used to make statements about the generality of the effects and to help interpret differences in the results obtained by different measures. In the second study, people are asked to produce accounts of helping behaviours they have recently engaged in. Respondents then classify their behaviours using the taxonomy, revealing the naturally occurring distribution of helping activities in their everyday lives. The third study deals with norms and expectations of behaviour held for types of helping from different regions of the multidimensional helping space. Questionnaire role-playing data reveal differences in the expectations people hold for different types of helping, as well as significant interactions between personal characteristics and preferences for certain types of helping.

The final chapter contains three sections. The first one explores the implications of the helping taxonomy for theory construction in the social psychology of helping, in three ways: (1) establishing the limits of validity or relevance domains for the competing theories; (2) comparing the results of empirical studies to resolve apparent contradictions in the literature; and (3) investigating person-by-situation interactions in the explanation of helping behaviour. Examples are taken both from the existing body of literature and studies completed for this volume, to illustrate the main points. The second section extends the uses for the taxonomic approach into applications, addressing the connections between this approach and insights into the nature of professional helping and the helping pro-fessional. The final section returns to the larger issues in social psycho-logical research and theory construction which were initially raised in the present chapter. An assessment is made of the generalizability of the taxonomic approach to other fields of inquiry, its limitations, and the priority of pre-theoretical organizing research in social psychology today.

2

A Cognitively-based Taxonomy of Helping

P. R. AMATO and P. PEARCE

IN THE first chapter of this volume it was argued that an organizational framework would help to establish the limits of empirical and theoretical generalizations, allow the comparison and interpretation of research findings, and assist in the planning of future studies. There are several types of taxonomies or organizational schemes which could be used for this purpose. For example, the type of help needed could form the basis of a category scheme. Following this strategy, Schreiber and Glidewell (1978) divided help-giving into emotional support, advice and economic action (see Gottlieb, 1978 for a similar scheme). Staub (1978) attempted an organizational model based upon stimulus characteristics of situations which determine the elicitation of helping responses. A different method is that of Wispé (1972) who attempted a taxonomy based upon an analysis of the meanings of major helping terms. Alternatively, the physical setting in which help is required could be the focus of an organizing scheme with emphasis being placed either on the physical properties of the situation (Barker, 1968) or on the emotion-eliciting qualities of the environment (Mehrabian and Russell, 1974). However, these approaches will not be adopted in the present study since it is argued here that one needs to adopt a holistic approach and consider as many parameters of the situation as possible when constructing the taxonomy.

A useful concept in this context is that of a social episode (Forgas, 1980). According to Forgas, episodes are cognitive representations of stereotypical interaction sequences. Episodes constitute perceived units in the behavioural stream because of their symbolic, temporal and often physical boundaries. The value of using the concept of episodes in the present context is that it encompasses the entirety of the interaction sequence between recipient and helper. Such a general approach includes the terms of helping need, helping behaviour and helping situation in one general concept. This avoids focusing on narrow aspects of helping such as the seriousness of the situation or the type of help needed and favours a multidimensional view of the interaction sequence as a whole. In addition, if one considers the helping episodes which researchers have studied, it should be possible to categorize these episodes in the same quantitative way as has been effected for episodes in general.

The quantitative technique used to study episodes has typically involved an explicitly cognitive approach using judgemental ratings from sets of subjects. Techniques such as multidimensional scaling are then used to identify the underlying perceptual dimensions subjects use to distinguish between episodes. Since this approach is not without its critics (cf. Argyle, 1979) some justification for this cognitive approach to the development of a taxonomy is required.

The use of a cognitive approach in this area has been criticized on a number of grounds. On the one hand, it is argued that people have limited access to their cognitive processes. Consequently it can be proposed that in many studies research participants have unintentionally provided investigators with material of an artefactual nature. Secondly, previous studies of episodes using multidimensional scaling approaches have sometimes resulted in the spatial juxtaposition of episodes of a somewhat different nature. For example, Forgas (1980) found, in the study of the social life of university rugby-team members, that sherry parties, tutorials and discussing match tactics were perceived as highly similar types of episodes. The value of providing such a general level of similarity as presented above has been questioned, since it is argued that the goals, required behaviour and social rules of such episodes are so different as to obviate the value of discussing similarities.

A careful examination of both of these arguments reveals that they are somewhat limited when applied to the cognitive approach to helping adopted here. The view that actors have limited access to their cognitive processes stems most directly from the work of Nisbett and Wilson (1977). They argue that individuals cannot account for their internal mental processes since they are often unaware of important stimuli, unaware of the way they are responding and unaware of stimulus-response connections. Nisbett and Wilson point out that people can be fluent in talking about their cognitive processes and under a limited range of conditions may be accurate in their comments. It is suggested that such accuracy of verbal reports exists only when influential stimuli are salient and plausible causes of the responses they produce.

This argument represents a serious objection to the view that subjects know all the answers about their own behaviour and cognitions, and suggests that psychological research must not rely too exclusively on the participant's accounting of behaviour. However, for the present purposes it must be noted that the crux of Nisbett and Wilson's argument is directed towards cognitive processes, not cognitive products. This necessitates a close examination of the task subjects are required to perform when their views of helping episodes are being considered. In the present study, information about cognitive processes is not being sought. Rather, the research requires people to compare "cognitive products" and the "discovery" method of multidimensional scaling is used to elicit possible structural and processing explanations inherent in these comparisons. That is, subjects are not being asked to give a full account of why two helping episodes are defined differently. Instead they will be asked to comment on the degree to which two episodes differ.

In summary, the position that a cognitive approach to helping is suspect because people have limited access to their cognitive processes, does not apply directly to the present approach where cognitive products rather than cognitive processes are the focus of the study.

Argyle's (1979) criticism that the dimensional interpretations provided by multidimensional scaling studies of episodes are so general as to be pointless, loses its force when one focuses on a specific set of episodes. Whereas Forgas and others were concerned to document the full social repertoire of their participants, the present study has the more limited aim of understanding the cognitive representations of a small set of social episodes: those concerned with helping. It is argued that within this more limited set of episodes, superficiality of the distinctions articulated by the participants will be less problematic. The situation under study may be seen as analogous to the elicitation of constructs within the Kelly grid frame of analysis. As Collett (1979) and others have argued, finer-grained distinctions are provided when participants discriminate among elements which are quite similar in nature. If researchers concentrate on the upper echelons of the construct hierarchy, relatively trivial distinctions in the individual's view of his social life appear (e.g. male versus female). However, at lower levels of the construct hierarchy where the elements are highly similar (e.g. the distinctions among three girlfriends), more personal and informative constructs are revealed (e.g. accepts me as I am–wants me to be something different). In order to provide a good general overview of helping it is desirable that the present approach offers participants the opportunity to distinguish between both highly similar and highly dissimilar types of helping. This in turn focuses attention on the sampling procedure used in selecting the helping episodes. This will be dealt with in some detail in the methodological section of this chapter.

There are also many positive arguments which support the choice of an explicitly cognitive approach for a taxonomy of helping. For example, such an approach is broadly consistent with what Backman (1979) has described as the "cognitive revolution in social psychology". This revolution has many origins with notable contributions from symbolic interactionism, phenomenology and ethnomethodology (Blumer, 1969; Schutz, 1967; Garfinkel, 1967, 1973).

The central emphasis of these cognitive approaches is that the individual reacts to his own construction of social reality. However, this emphasis on the actor's definition of the social situation is not totally individualistic, since individuals are influenced in their definition of situations by their culture and social groups. Such approaches to social life suggest that shared perspectives and similar definitions of social episodes are likely to characterize the cognitive appraisals of similar groups of people. Such shared perspectives or intersubjectivities can be seen as the building blocks for the commonality and normative behaviour which takes place in social episodes. In short, if research participants define a situation in a common way it is likely that their response to that situation will be similar.

Backman (1979) and Mixon (1974) have reinterpreted some previous experimental work with these kinds of cognitive explanations. They argue that researchers have not paid sufficient attention to the problem of the subjective meaning of the experimental situation by research subjects. Mixon's (1974) reinterpretation of Milgram's (1963) obedience studies is a good example. Mixon argued that Milgram's experimental situation seems quite clear to outsiders, yet subjects actually in the experiment were highly confused by one aspect of the situation: the experimenter's total lack of concern with the victim's distress. Mixon's role-playing re-enactments of the experiment suggest that subjects administered severe shock because, in the extreme ambiguity of the situation, they defined the situation as an experiment in which normal safeguards only appeared to have broken down. Subjects who believed they were really hurting the victim disobeyed the experimenter. The point that Mixon and Backman seek to emphasize is that many investigators have failed to perceive that their study could and was being interpreted by subjects in non-obvious ways.

Some opponents of an explicitly cognitive approach to helping would argue that researchers recognize the role of subjects' definitions of situations and adequately consider this perspective by reporting manipulation checks on their experimental situation. Provided that research participants are given adequate scope to express their genuine interpretations of the situation, this checking procedure is highly desirable but unfortunately it is still often accompanied by a highly deterministic view of human action. There is little point in considering the subject's view of the research situation and then failing to consider the decisions and behavioural outcomes inherent in these views. More simply, most manipulation checks report mean data, implying that subjects on average interpreted the situation in the intended fashion. Having thus dismissed any qualms about the experimental interpretation, many researchers then proceed to explore their data as if subjects were totally uniform in their responses to the manipulation. It can be argued that this procedure offers an inadequate account of the role of cognitive processes influencing behaviour and considerably reduces the amount of variance accounted for in the final analysis. Accordingly, while manipulation checks can be seen as acknowledgement of the importance of cognitive processes, it is argued that they have been used in a superficial manner and do not do justice to the cognitive perspective under discussion.

The preceding commentary has served to clarify a number of central perspectives in this volume. Taken together with the material on taxonomies in Chapter 1, the essential approach of the present study will be part of a program of studies which (1) take a cognitive perspective on helping, (2) attempt to derive a taxonomy of helping, (3) use the concept of a helping episode as the unit of analysis and (4) sample the range of helping episodes studied as broadly as possible.

Method

The aim of the first study was to use multidimensional scaling techniques to discover the implicit criteria people use to distinguish between instances of helping. The first step in this procedure was to select a sample of helping episodes. In many multidimensional scaling studies, this is a crucial problem, for without a listing of all the elements of the population, it is difficult to know whether one has sampled from the entire range of a given behavioural domain (Frederiksen, 1972). This is precisely the case with a form of behaviour such as helping. To make the results directly relevant to the literature on helping, it was decided to make use of the actual measures of helping from past studies conducted by social psychologists. There is no guarantee, of course, that this is a good representation of the full range of possible forms of helping, but it served as a starting point (this issue is discussed in detail in Chapter 3).

A list of well over 100 helping behaviours was compiled by scanning several hundred articles published in major journals such as the following: *Journal of Personality and Social Psychology, Journal of Social Psychology, Journal of Experimental Social Psychology, Journal of Applied Social Psychology, European Journal of Social Psychology, Sociometry,* and *Personality and Social Pschology Bulletin.* This list, however, was too long for multidimensional scaling procedures, so it was pruned to a total of 62 items by removing those forms of helping with substantial overlap with another item (for example, donating anonymously to two different charity appeals). Many of the studies used identical or nearly identical measures of helping.

These measures of helping were then summarized as brief helping episodes for presentations to respondents. An example would be "Mailing a lost letter that you have found on the street for the person who wrote it, even though you do not know him/her". The complete list of 62 helping episodes, as given to our subjects, is displayed in Table 2.1.

The respondents in this study were 72 male and female first-year students enrolled in the Department of Behavioural Sciences at James Cook University of North Queensland who volunteered for this project. These students ranged in age from 17 to 50 with a median age of 19. Thirty-four percent of these people were over 25.

Respondents were seated in rooms containing between 10 and 20 people and were given the list of 62 helping episodes and a grid sheet for their responses. They were instructed to read selected pairs of episodes and decide whether they involved basically similar or dissimilar kinds of helping. They then rated the degree of similarity between the two on a scale from 1 to 5 on their grid sheet. Due to the large number of pairs this procedure generates (1891 altogether), any particular rater was required to rate only a subsample of the pairs (about 300 ratings). This task took most people about 1 hour to complete. Thus, it took a total of six people to complete one matrix of 1891 similarity ratings, with each possible pair of stimuli being rated by a total of 12 people. These data were then aggregated and the mean rating for each stimulus pair served as input into the multidimensional scaling program.

Since every rater did not judge every possible pair of stimuli, and because every pair was rated by a total of only 12 subjects, a check was made to see how much agreement existed between the similarity ratings given by different raters. A sub-sample of 12 raters was chosen from the 72, and a random sample of 100 stimulus pairs which the 12 raters had all rated in common was also selected. The 12 sets of ratings for these 100 stimulus pairs were then intercorrelated using Spearman's rank-order correlation coefficient. The intercorrelations between the 12 raters ranged from 0.02 to 0.65 with a mean coefficient of 0.34 ($p < 0.05$). Eighty-nine percent of the inter-rater coefficients were significant at the 0.05 level. Thus, substantial variation was exhibited between raters, with some agreeing at a fairly high level and others showing little agreement. Nevertheless, none of the correlations were negative, and the average pair of raters agreed at a moderate, and statistically significant, level.

The reliability of the ratings improved when the data were aggregated for groups of subjects. The same 12 raters were randomly divided into two groups of six subjects each and the mean rating given by each group of six on the same 100 stimulus pairs was calculated. These two sets of means were correlated, yielding a correlation of 0.75 ($p < 0.001$). Overall, there appeared to be enough consistency in the data to serve as meaningful input into a multidimensional scaling program.

The data were analysed with the MINISSA program from the MDS(X) series. MINISSA was originated by E. E. Roskam and J. C. Lingoes (1977) and consists of an algorithm to find the coordinates of a set of points (corresponding, in this case, to the 62 helping stimuli) in an r-dimensional space such that the distances between the points is of the same rank order

TABLE 2.1   *List of helping episodes as presented to subjects*

1. You give what change you have to a student who approaches you in a library asking for 50 cents to make some xerox copies.
2. At the request of your instructor you volunteer to give time to a publicity campaign to acquaint the community with the role of the university.
3. Donating food to an appeal for the poor.
4. Volunteering to collate materials for your instructor to use in a course you are taking (the instructor has asked for volunteers).
5. Stopping to pick up a hitch hiker standing along the side of the road.
6. Sharing a small amount of money you have just won in a game with a friend of yours.
7. Mailing a wallet containing a small amount of money back to its owner after you have found it lying on the street.
8. While filling out a questionnaire for a research organization you hear two children in the next room begin to fight; you go in to break up the fight because it sounds like one child is getting badly beaten.
9. Making a phone call for a woman to her husband after she has approached you in a shopping centre claiming to have just sprained her ankle.
10. Mailing a package for a person you do not know after s/he has approached you on the street claiming that s/he has to catch a train.
11. You are working in a small shop and point out to a customer who has just purchased something that s/he has given you too much money for the item.
12. You are asked by a pedestrian if you have dropped some money on the ground which s/he has just found; since you haven't, you reply that it is not yours.
13. Giving the time to a stranger on the street.
14. Agreeing to give a new blouse a number of washings as part of a testing program for a new product conducted by a market research organization.
15. While walking through a building you see a technician receive a powerful electric shock while working on some electrical equipment; you help the unconscious person by giving direct help or by calling for aid.
16. Stopping your car to help a motorist standing by his/her car on the side of the road with a flat tyre.
17. You agree to be interviewed by a researcher who presents him/herself at your front door.
18. A person you have met once, briefly asks you to help him/her by distributing political attitude questionnaires to people; you agree.
19. After taking part in a psychology experiment, the researcher asks you to stay on and perform a numbering task as a favour; you agree.
20. Saving milk cartons, washing them out, and turning them in to a group of university students collecting them for an art project.
21. While waiting for a bus you see a person fall over clutching his knee in pain; you run over to help.
22. Helping a stranger pick up computer cards after you have accidentally knocked them out of his/her hands while walking down the street.
23. Helping a young child with a task that is too difficult.
24. Sharing a small amount of food (nuts) with an acquaintance of yours.
25. Donating money to a charity box.
26. Calling a garage for a stranger who has accidentally called you with his/her last 10-cent piece and has a car that will not start.
27. Helping a stranger pick up pencils s/he has dropped in an elevator you are both riding.
28. As part of a study, you are discussing problems of urban living with another student over an intercom; when the student tells you s/he is suffering from an epileptic seizure, you rush in to help.
29. Stopping to help a lost child who is crying, alone on the street.
30. While playing a game involving the betting of money, you give another player (who you have never met before) who is almost broke enough money to keep playing (one dollar).
31. At the request of an acquaintance you volunteer time to bind storybooks for poor children.

TABLE 2.1   *(Cont.)*

32. Filling out a questionnaire for a fellow student who is doing a study.
33. Mailing a lost letter that you have found on the street for the person who wrote it, even though you do not know him/her.
34. Volunteering to participate in a psychology experiment after your lecturer has asked for volunteers.
35. Volunteering to counsel high-school students after your lecturer has asked for volunteers.
36. Donating blood to a blood bank.
37. You are participating in an experiment in which you receive a mild electric shock; you are in control of the level of shock that both you and your partner will receive; you set you partner's level very low even though it means your level of shocks will be higher (and more painful).
38. A woman in a discount store asks you to give her a hand with a stuck shopping cart.
39. Writing your favourite colour for a student who approaches you in a shopping mall and is working on a class project.
40. Giving change for a 20-cent piece to a stranger who approaches you on the street.
41. You point the way for a stranger who has approached you on the street asking for directions.
42. Helping a stranger look for a lost contact lens on the hallway floor of a university building.
43. While filling out a questionnaire for a market research organization, you hear the investigator fall off a chair in the next room; you rush in to help.
44. Giving 20 cents to a stranger who approaches you on the street claiming to need the money for bus fare.
45. You overhear one person talking to another person giving directions; since you realize the directions are incorrect, you step over and correct him.
46. You agree to chaperone a small group of children from the juvenile detention centre on a trip to the zoo.
47. Donating time to spend with a mentally retarded boy.
48. Helping a person pick up groceries that have fallen out of the bottom of a broken bag outside a supermarket (you don't know the person).
49. While in a waiting room a stranger comes through with a big armload of books; you get up and open the closed door for this person.
50. You are approached by a deaf person who hands you a note asking that you make a phone call for him/her; you make the call.
51. Coming to the aid of a person who collapses, apparently unconscious, while riding a bus.
52. An appeal is made to you from a medical person to donate bone marrow for a seriously ill patient (a stranger); although it is a painful process, you agree.
53. Volunteering to contribute time to read to a blind university student.
54. You stop to help a person on the street, who is reading a city map and is obviously lost, by giving directions.
55. You work extra hard for your supervisor at work, knowing that s/he is eligible for a prize if productivity is up.
56. Informing a passerby on the street that s/he has unknowingly dropped a small package.
57. Turning the lights off on a parked car which has an open window (you don't know the owner).
58. Coming to the aid of a stranger lying on the sidewalk ahead of you, clutching his/her chest.
59. On a university campus, a stranger approaches you and asks you to return some books to the library; although it is out of your way, you agree.
60. A woman approaches you on the street and aks you to give her a hand getting her male friend to a first-aid station; you agree.
61. Giving money to a multiple sclerosis fund when a collector knocks on your door.
62. Breaking up a fight between two university students.

as the (dis)similarity ratings between the stimuli. MINISSA is a non-metric smallest-space analysis which reproduces the underlying structure inherent in a set of data.

Results and Discussion

Solutions were obtained in 5, 4, 3, 2 and 1 dimensions. The stress levels for the solutions were, respectively: 0.12, 0.14, 0.18, 0.26 and 0.43. The three-dimensional solution was chosen as the optimal one because the stress level was acceptable and the obtained configuration could be interpreted easily. Adding the fourth and fifth dimensions reduced the stress level marginally and did not add to the interpretability of the solution.

The coordinates of the 62 helping stimuli along the three dimensions are shown in Table 2.2. Abbreviated labels have been used to identify the helping episodes. Since 62 episodes are difficult to plot in three dimensions in a single figure, a representative sample of 20 stimuli from every area of the three-dimensional space was chosen for graphic representation. These data appear in Figure 2.1. Readers can plot in any other helping episode of interest by using the coordinates supplied in Table 2.2.

Following a procedure suggested by Kruskal and Wish (1978) a second and third configuration were generated by rerunning the MINISSA program with subsamples of 25 and 21 stimuli. The result was essentially the same in both cases, with stimuli appearing in about the same area in the space relative to each other. In both cases the three-dimensional solution was the best, using the criteria of stress level and interpretability.

Using a neighbourhood interpretation, certain clusterings of stimuli can be noted in the three-dimensional space when all 62 stimuli are plotted (these clusters are not readily apparent in Figure 2.1 due to the small number of stimuli plotted). The first cluster consists of episodes 8, 15, 21, 28, 37, 43, 51, 58, 60 and 62, all representing situations of some seriousness. Hence, this grouping can be thought of as an "emergency intervention" cluster. A second cluster consists of episodes 2, 4, 14, 18, 17, 19, 20, 31, 32, 34, 35, 46, 47 and 53. These episodes all involve formal, planned, organizational forms of helping, and could be labelled "formal, organizational helping". The third cluster is made up of episodes 5, 9, 10, 13, 16, 22, 26, 27, 33, 40, 41, 42, 45, 48, 49, 50, 56 and 57. This large cluster could be described as "informal, casual, everyday help to strangers". Finally, a fourth cluster consists of episodes 1, 3, 6, 7, 11, 12, 24, 25, 30, 36, 44 and 61, all forms of helping which involve giving material assistance to people. Hence, this could be labelled a "donating and sharing" cluster.

However, after closer inspection, it was decided that a dimensional interpretation might be more appropriate. Accordingly, attention was directed toward labelling the dimensions which appeared to run through

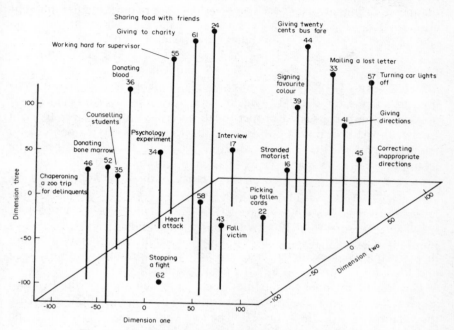

Fig. 2.1   Three-dimensional representation of episode space.

the multidimensional space. Although the axes in MINISSA are arbitrary and may be rotated, the three dimensions seemed easily interpretable without rotation. While we had intuitive hunches about the labelling of the dimensions, it was decided to check on these labels empirically.

To do this, judges were recruited to rate the 62 helping episodes on a number of 7-point bipolar scales which could then be fitted as vectors through the multidimensional space via regression procedures. The scales were chosen either because they seemed reasonable interpretations of the dimensions or were suggested by the literature on helping as being of importance. These scales are listed in Table 2.3. For example, the seventh scale, "feel sympathy for the person–feel little sympathy for the person", was suggested by Wispé's (1978) discussion of the role of sympathy in helping, and number 10, "costs me little to help–costs me a lot to help", was suggested by Piliavin and Piliavin's discussion of the role of cost in helping (1972).

The judges consisted of 45 female and male second-year students at James Cook University of North Queensland. Their ages ranged from 18 to 52 with a median age of 22. These people were given a list of the 62 helping episodes and a series of rating sheets with the bipolar scales listed. They then rated the 62 helping episodes on each of the 16 scales. Due to the large number of ratings involved, each person rated only about one-third of the 62 episodes. Each episode was rated by a total of 15 people. The mean ratings on each of the 16 scales were then computed for each episode.

These mean ratings were used as input into the PREFMAP program. PREFMAP was originated by Carroll and Chang and is part of the MDS(X) series (1977). The vector model, available in PREFMAP, was used to analyse the data. The vector model uses an algorithm suited for assessing whether a scaled property can be represented as a vector in a Euclidean space of points possessing that property to varying degrees. In addition to finding the "best vector" and providing direction cosines to fix its orientation in the space, PREFMAP computes the correlation between projected values of each point on the vector and the input values from the scale itself. This latter quantity is the best indicator of how adequate the vector representation is for the scale concerned. The coordinates of the 62 helping episodes on the three dimensions as supplied by the MINISSA program were also used as input. The fourth dimension, although not interpretable, was extracted first, a procedure recommended by Kruskal and Wish (1978) to "clean up" the configuration.

The direction cosines for the fitted vector representations of the 16 scales and the correlation of the scale means with the projections of the stimuli on the vectors are given in Table 2.3. The two scales which serve as the best interpretations of the first dimension are planned help–spontaneous help (direction cosine = 0.93, $r = 0.77$) and formal help–informal help (direction cosine = 0.89, $r = 0.69$). Inspection of the configuration reveals that episodes such as "chaperoning a group of juvenile delinquents on a zoo trip" and "volunteering for a psychology experiment after your lecturer has asked for volunteers" are at one pole of this dimension and episodes such as "giving directions to a stranger" and "turning off the lights on a parked car" are at the other pole.

The situation is serious–situation is not serious scale appears to be the best interpretation for the second dimension (direction cosine = 0.98, $r = 0.70$). Other scales in approximate alignment with the second axis, and with reasonably high correlations are difficult to do–not difficult to do, don't know what to do–know what to do, and feel sympathy for the person–feel little sympathy for the person. Episodes like "helping a heart-attack victim" and "donating bone marrow for a seriously ill medical patient" appear at one pole of this dimension and episodes like "writing your favourite colour for a student working on a class project" and "mailing a lost letter" appear at the other pole of this dimension.

The third dimension is characterized by episodes such as "picking up dropped computer cards" and "breaking up a fight" on the one hand while the other pole of the dimension involves episodes such as "sharing food with friends" and "donating to charity". Giving what I have–doing what I can describes this dimension (direction cosine $= -0.94$, $r = 0.71$), with indirect intervention–direct intervention (direction cosine $= -0.71$, $r = 0.70$) also serving as a reasonable interpretation.

Overall, this suggests a three-fold structure of helping. First, there is spontaneous, informal versus planned, formal help. Second, there is serious versus non-serious help. Third, there is doing, direct help versus giving, indirect help. The second dimension appears to relate to the need of the recipient, while the third dimension relates to the type of response required from the helper. The first dimension characterizes the type of situation in which helping occurs, that is it distinguishes helping which occurs spontaneously, with little prior warning, in casual and informal settings, from help which has been planned ahead of time by the helper, has less immediacy, and occurs in more formal, structured settings.

The seriousness dimension is the one which has appeared most often in the literature on helping. Both Bar-tal (1976) and Latané and Darley (1970) distinguish serious, emergency helping from less serious, everyday helping. Furthermore, the seriousness dimension has been empirically investigated in a number of previous studies (Ashton and Severy, 1976; Staub and Baer, 1974; Shotland and Huston, 1979). While it has been recognized that the type of assistance required is also an important variable, the giving versus doing distinction, as such, has not received much attention in the literature on helping. However, a number of studies have compared direct versus indirect forms of assistance (Schwartz and Clausen, 1970; Page, 1977). Very little research appears to have been directed toward the planned, formal versus spontaneous, informal dimension. It is probably the most surprising dimension to emerge from the present analysis. An article by Benson and his colleagues (1980), making reference to spontaneous versus nonspontaneous help, is one of the few to draw attention to this important distinction. Further investigations of differences between planned, formal types of helping and spontaneous, informal types of helping might generate interesting results, given the salience of this dimension for our subjects.

A Replication Study

Before continuing with this line of research, it was decided to see if the first study could be replicated using a different group of subjects, a somewhat different sample of helping episodes, and a different method of analysing the data. Accordingly, the sample of 62 helping episodes was stratified on the basis of the three dimensions, and a representative sample of 25 stimuli covering all regions of the multidimensional space was selected. Twenty student volunteers from the University of Queensland in Brisbane were

TABLE 2.2 *List of the sixty-two helping stimuli and their coordinates in the three-dimensional configuration*

	Dim. 1	Dim. 2	Dim. 3
1. Giving 50 cents for xerox copies	0.05	0.52	0.45
2. Time to a community campaign	−1.15	−0.03	−0.21
3. Donating food to the poor	−0.01	−0.43	0.81
4. Collating materials for a class	−1.09	0.41	−0.11
5. Picking up a hitch hiker	0.72	0.19	−0.10
6. Sharing money you won with friends	0.13	−0.17	0.96
7. Mailing a wallet to its owner	0.55	−0.06	0.47
8. Stopping children from fighting	0.57	−0.75	−0.51
9. Phoning for a sprained-ankle victim	0.52	−0.21	0.06
10. Mailing a package for a stranger	0.36	0.15	0.04
11. Returning an overpayment	0.92	0.18	0.76
12. Not claiming money lost by others	0.91	0.43	1.00
13. Giving the time	0.28	0.53	−0.18
14. Washing blouse in market research	−0.97	0.61	−0.46
15. Electric-shock victim	0.52	−0.97	−0.11
16. Helping stranded motorist	0.58	−0.09	−0.34
17. Interviewed by researcher	−0.64	0.72	−0.64
18. Distributing questionnaires	−0.91	0.29	−0.61
19. Numbering task after experiment	−0.87	0.35	−0.31
20. Saving cartons for art students	−0.67	0.42	0.14
21. Helping someone fallen over	0.52	−0.62	−0.26
22. Picking up computer cards	0.32	0.07	−0.94
23. Helping a child with a hard task	0.05	−0.03	−0.69
24. Sharing food with friends	−0.18	−0.18	1.17
25. Donating money to a charity box	−0.39	0.13	1.01
26. Calling a garage; wrong number	0.33	0.15	0.17
27. Picking up pencils	0.56	0.43	−0.55
28. Helping an epileptic	0.31	−0.93	−0.54
29. Assisting a lost child	0.44	−0.36	−0.52
30. Funding a fellow player; card game	0.08	0.48	1.02
31. Binding storybooks for poor kids	−0.80	−0.26	0.07
32. Filling out a questionnaire	−0.74	0.76	−0.12
33. Mailing a lost letter	0.49	0.57	0.31
34. Volunteering for an experiment	−1.11	0.25	−0.34
35. Counselling high-school students	−1.15	−0.15	−0.43
36. Donating blood	−0.53	−0.77	0.78
37. Lowering partner's shock level	0.01	−1.14	0.85
38. Hand with stuck shopping cart	0.26	0.32	−0.56
39. Colour request	−0.21	0.97	−0.27
40. Giving change for a phone call	0.34	0.86	0.12
41. Giving directions	0.57	0.56	−0.24
42. Looking for lost contact lens	0.41	0.13	−0.41
43. Helping a fall victim	0.54	−0.87	−0.47
44. Giving 20 cents for bus fare	0.39	0.33	0.75
45. Correcting inappropriate directions	1.14	0.18	−0.33
46. Chaperone delinquents on zoo trip	−1.00	−0.73	−0.03
47. Time with mentally retarded boy	−0.82	−0.87	0.18
48. Picking up fallen groceries	0.61	0.27	−0.63
49. Opening a door for someone	0.41	0.66	−0.38
50. Phone call for deaf person	0.02	−0.11	−0.05
51. Aiding an unconscious person	0.37	−1.01	−0.02
52. Donating bone marrow to patient	−0.42	−1.25	0.29

TABLE 2.2 *(cont.)*

		Dim. 1	Dim. 2	Dim. 3
53.	Reading to a blind student	-0.64	-0.35	0.04
54.	Aiding a lost person	0.22	0.54	-0.32
55.	Working hard for your supervisor	-1.15	0.53	0.47
56.	Information about a dropped package	0.72	0.60	0.10
57.	Turning lights off; parked car	0.68	0.78	0.11
58.	Heart-attack victim	0.36	-1.04	-0.14
59.	Returning books to the library	-0.16	0.40	0.19
60.	Helping a man to first aid	0.01	-0.60	0.20
61.	Money to Multiple Sclerosis fund	-0.52	0.03	0.99
62.	Breaking up a fight	-0.16	-0.85	-1.30

recruited to give similarity ratings between all possible pairs of stimuli. The similarity ratings generated by these subjects were analysed with the INDSCAL program (Individual Differences Multidimensional Scaling). INDSCAL was originated by Carroll and Chang (1977) and is part of the MDS (X) series. The INDSCAL model is based upon the assumption that the attribute dimensions underlying perceptions of a sample of stimuli may have differential relevance to different individuals. The model uses a complete set of judgements from each subject to produce a unique group stimulus space, the dimensions of which are said to correspond to meaningful psychological dimensions which are usually interpretable without further rotation. INDSCAL also calculates a set of dimension weights reflecting the salience of the various dimensions to each individual.

The INDSCAL program produced a three-dimensional configuration

TABLE 2.3 *Bipolar scales used for dimensional interpretation, direction cosines for each dimension, and the correlation between observed and expected scale values*

Rating scale	Dim. 1	Dim. 2	Dim. 3	Correlation
1. Planned help–spontaneous help	0.93	0.23	-0.28	0.77
2. Formal help–informal help	0.89	0.45	0.04	0.69
3. Self-initiated help–other initiated help	-0.89	0.45	-0.01	0.47
4. Situation is serious–situation is not serious	-0.19	0.98	0.10	0.70
5. Difficult to do–not difficult to do	0.60	0.77	0.21	0.77
6. Know what to do–don't know what to do	-0.47	-0.81	-0.35	0.71
7. Feel sympathy for the person–feel no sympathy	-0.46	0.89	-0.01	0.67
8. Everyday occurrence–unusual occurrence	-0.43	-0.82	-0.37	0.56
9. Costs me a lot of help–costs me little to help	0.68	0.65	-0.35	0.67
10. Masculine help–feminine help	-0.64	0.67	0.37	0.50
11. In control of situation–not in control	-0.12	-0.97	-0.20	0.33
12. Feel free to help–feel compelled to help	-0.54	-0.65	-0.54	0.46
13. *Giving* what I have–*doing* what I can	0.32	0.10	-0.94	0.71
14. Indirect intervention–direct intervention	0.59	-0.38	-0.71	0.70
15. Active help–passive help	-0.27	0.43	0.86	0.59
16. Makes me feel good–makes me feel bad	-0.67	-0.35	-0.71	0.28

which accounted for 33 percent of the variance in the subjects' similarity ratings. Although the percent of variance accounted for was somewhat low, the solution was strikingly similar to the one generated in the first study, with stimuli falling in about the same area of the three-dimensional space relative to each other. As a check on the interpretability of the new configuration, the bipolar ratings obtained in the first study were input into a PREFMAP program along with the coordinates of the 25 stimuli from the three-dimensional INDSCAL space.

The planned help–spontaneous help and the formal help–informal help scales appeared to be the best interpretations for the second dimension, with respective direction cosines of -0.91 and -0.81 and correlations of 0.72 and 0.67. The first dimension was well represented by the serious–not serious scale (direction cosine $= 0.89$, $r = 0.70$), and by don't know what to do–know what to do (direction cosine $= 0.86$, $r = 0.72$) and cost a lot to help–costs little to help (direction cosine $= 0.84$, $r = 0.78$). The third dimension was best represented by three scales: giving what I have–doing what I can, indirect intervention–direct intervention, and passive help–active help (direction cosines, respectively, were 0.84, 0.99 and 0.76). However, the PREFMAP correlations for these last three scales were rather low: 0.51, 0.56 and 0.49, respectively. These low correlations may reflect an atrophied range of helping episodes due to the decreased number of stimuli.

While the subjects revealed a certain amount of individual variation in the salience of the three dimensions, these differences in dimensional weights did not appear to be related to any of the demographic variables included in the study. (The topic of intergroup differences in perceptions of helping is addressed in detail in Chapter 4.)

All in all, there appeared to be enough consistency between the results of the first and second study to warrant the further elaboration of this taxonomic model. An important question, however, refers to the original sampling of helping episodes. The results of any data-reduction techniques, such as multidimensional scaling, are limited by the range of data one begins with. The present sample of helping episodes was derived from the social psychological literature on helping behaviour. Can one assume that social psychologists, after more than a decade of research in this area, have adequately covered the entire range of different type of helping? Or have researchers, for one reason or another, left out or seriously understudied certain kinds of helping? This seems likely, for the tradition of helping research in social psychology has mainly limited itself to short-term helping between strangers, and has had little to say about long-term helping in relationships between kin, friends and work associates. If there are major omissions in the helping literature, then the results of our first taxonomic studies may be seriously limited. It is with this question that the third chapter is concerned.

3

An Unstudied Type of Helping

M. SMITHSON and P. R. AMATO

Rationale and Method for the Second Study

IN ANY attempt to obtain an overview of the field of helping studies, the question must eventually be asked whether social psychologists have covered all main types of helping in their research. In a cognitively based approach such as ours, this question is crucial, since it is possible that people may distinguish among types of helping not dealt with in the social psychological literature. The study in this chapter entails a search for and discovery of the kinds of helping situations which have been neglected by social psychologists, and the characteristics which distinguish them in people's minds from their more well-studied counterparts. The objectives here were two-fold: first, to arrive at a truly representative sample of helping situations; and second, to determine whether any definable characteristics distinguish the unstudied kinds of helping from those treated in the literature.

A "representative" sample here means a collection of helping examples which contains at least one good example of every major type of helping recognized by ordinary people. To do this required a reasonably comprehensive typology of the sort used in everyday thought. Popular typologies usually are reflected in natural languages, often by categorical labels. Thus, the initial steps in the search for unstudied helping episodes involved extracting a list of types from a dictionary, with the aid of a Thesaurus. The list was then pruned for obvious synonyms, resulting in a refined list of some 93 words or phrases, most of them verbs, describing various helping actions. Subjects were asked to rate helping episodes from the social psychological literature for how good an example each was of the terms in the list. Those terms for which no good examples were provided would then stand out as neglected varieties of helping. This procedure is explained in detail below.

To operationalize the concept of a "good example", fuzzy-set concepts were invoked in the construction of the rating tasks. A fuzzy-set is a set whose boundaries are not hard-edged as in classical set theory, but instead blurred, so that elements may belong partially to such a set rather than belonging completely or not at all (for an introduction to fuzzy-set theory and concepts, see Zadeh, 1965, or Kaufmann, 1975). Studies in cognitive psychology (Rosch, 1973, Kochen, 1975; and Zysno, 1979) and cognitive anthropology (Kay and McDaniel, 1975; and Kempton, 1978) have provided evidence that at least some category schemes used by people contain this kind of set, and that generally the more complex the referent set the more likely that the categories will be blurred and overlap one another. Because they permit partial belonging to a category and intercategory overlap, fuzzy-set concepts are well suited to defining such notions as "good example" and "poor example" in a systematic fashion.

Subjects were asked to rate each helping episode on a scale from 0 to 10 in terms of how good an example it was of every helping type on the list. In the instructions, subjects were told that a rating of 10 indicated that the example was an excellent one, while 0 indicated that the helping episode was not at all an example of the type with which it was compared.

Following the work of Lakoff (1973) and Kempton (1978), descriptive phrases were used to assist subjects and researchers in systematically linking the 0 to 10 scale with intuitive notions about degree of membership in a category. The phrases and their attendant rating-values are tabulated below:

> 0 = Not at all an example of _____
> 2 = In a way an example of _____
> 4 = Sort of an example of _____
> 6 = Generally an example of _____
> 8 = Definitely an example of _____
> 10 = An excellent example of _____

Ratings were entered into matrices with helping episodes cross-classified with types. Because of the large number of ratings required, the list of types was randomly divided into seven sets of terms, each of which had one term in common with every other set for the purpose of checking for equivalence between groups of raters. A total of 35 subjects completed ratings in this phase of the study on a sample of 25 helping episodes from the social psychological literature. Thus, for instance, a subject might be asked to consider a description of a helping episode such as "Picking up pencils for a stranger who has dropped them in an elevator you both are riding", and to rate how good an example this episode is of the term "assisting". If the subject thinks that this episode is definitely an example of assisting, but not a really excellent example, then he might assign a rating of 8. On the other hand, if asked to rate this episode as an example of the term "forewarning", then the subject might decide that the episode is in no way an example of forewarning and therefore give it a rating of 0. A sample rating form is displayed in Appendix 1.

The 25 helping episodes were a representative sample of the original 62 compiled for the study described in Chapter 2. The rating tasks required of the subjects were too lengthy for them to be able to complete the entire list of 62 episodes so the list had to be pruned drastically. The 25 episodes for this study were selected in such a way as to ensure that a MDS run on them alone reproduced the original space that emerged in the previous study. That the space was adequately reproduced was confirmed by computing a Spearman's Rho between the derived interpoint distances for these 25 points from the original MINISSA solution and from a MINISSA run using the 25 alone. The correlation value was 0.94, indicating very good reproduction.

Redundant terms for pairs of subject groups were checked for inter-group agreement before further analysis was carried out. For each term shared by a pair of subject groups, the mean ratings were correlated between the two groups over the 25 stimuli. These correlations ranged in value from 0.72 to 0.94, indicating a sufficiently high agreement among groups to warrant analysing the dataset as a piece.

The mean ratings for each of the 25 helping episodes served as the basis for determining whether each type in the list had been adequately represented in the social psychological literature on helping. Now, we must recall that the rating-levels are associated with various natural language phrases that denote the degree of exemplarity ("sort of an example", "generally an example", etc.). These phrases are called "hedges" after Lakoff (1973), because of their use of modifiers to denote exemplarity. Because of the nature of the hedged phrases used in defining the goodness of an example, any term in the list which had a maximum rating of less than 4 was designated a "neglected" type, those which had a maximum rating of 6 or less were designated "marginally" represented, and the rest were defined as "well represented" in the sample. A list of the neglected and marginally represented terms is provided in Table 3.1.

TABLE 3.1 *Marginally represented helping terms*

inspiring	giving handouts[1]	consoling
forewarning	reinforcing	defending
nurturing[1]	encouraging	healing
mediating[1]	collaborating with	easing[2]
liberating	giving a blessing	ameliorating
doting on	solving	serving
exonerating	lending something	succouring
expediting[2]	reviving	

1 Refers to those terms for which good examples were found among the 62 helping forms used in the Pearce–Amato study.
2 Refers to terms whose meaning was not sufficiently clear to respondents to permit using them further in the study.

The 16 terms with the lowest ratings were chosen for membership in a reduced list from which new helping episodes would be generated to round out the sample of 25 episodes. For three additional terms, good examples were located in the original (Chapter 2) list of 62 episodes derived from the literature. Those terms were omitted from the list whose ratings were borderline (near 6). That the 16 new terms were not synonymous with one another was checked by using a measure for fuzzy category overlap developed by Smithson (1981), and the overlap values were sufficiently low (less than 0.25 in a range from 0 to 1) to confirm the intuition that none of these terms was redundant.

One example was constructed to represent each neglected type. For instance, "exonerating" was represented by a situation where "a student has been wrongly accused of a theft, and you provide evidence which clears him of the charge". Each example was tested for fit by having five judges rate its closeness to the relevant term on a scale from 1 to 10. Ratings for all 16 averaged above 8.5. A list of the 16 new helping episodes is given in Table 3.2, along with the original 25.

TABLE 3.2   *List of new and old helping forms*

*1   Taking care of a friend who has come down with the flu by bringing him/her hot food, extra blankets, Vitamin C, and filling the person's prescription.

*2   You tell your neighbour who doesn't have a radio that a cyclone is approaching the area.

*3   After a fellow student's ideas have been ridiculed in a tutorial discussion, you stand up and argue that the student is actually correct.

*4   You are working with others on a task you find interesting, and your enthusiasm influences them to become interested in it as well.

*5   You overhear a student crying because s/he failed an exam and you tell this person something which cheers him/her up.

*6   You call on a friend as a surprise, do his/her weekend housework, and then take him/her out for a fine evening meal.

*7   You give smelling salts to a person who has just fainted after winning a big prize in the lottery.

*8   You find a possum that has been caught in a trap, and you open the trap to let it go.

*9   Letting an acquaintance borrow a favourite book of yours to read.

*10   Every time you come home, you bring a small surprise gift for a young nephew.

*11   A frustrated Behavioural Science student has been struggling for 3 days with a computer program that will not run; after looking at it a while you point out the "bug" in the program.

*12   A student has been wrongly accused of a theft, and you provide evidence which clears him of the charge.

*13   A friend who is about to marry tells you that his/her parents disapprove; you tell your friend that you approve of their plan to marry.

*14   A friend has been faithfully observing a strict diet for the past few weeks, and you compliment her on her improved figure.

*15   Getting together with a fellow student to compare lecture notes in studying for an examination.

*16   A friend is studying for a difficult exam, and you tell him you think he'll do a good job on it.

TABLE 3.2   *(Cont.)*

---

17   You are asked by a pedestrian if you have dropped some money on the ground which s/he has found; since you haven't, you reply that it is not yours.
18   Stopping your car for a motorist standing by his/her car on the side of the road with a flat tyre.
19   You agree to be interviewed by a researcher who presents him/herself at the front door.
20   While waiting for a bus you see a person fall over clutching at his knee in pain; you run over to see what you can do.
21   Picking up a stranger's computer cards after you have accidentally knocked them out of his/her hands while walking down the street.
22   Helping a young child with a task which is too difficult.
23   Dividing a small amount of food (nuts) with an acquaintance of yours.
24   Picking up pencils for a stranger who has dropped them in an elevator you are both riding.
25   Stopping to attend to a lost child who is crying, alone on the street.
26   Mailing a lost letter that you have found on the street for the person who wrote it, even though you do not know that person.
27   Participating in a psychology experiment after your lecturer has asked for volunteers.
28   Agreeing to counsel high-school students after your lecturer has asked for volunteers.
29   You are participating in an experiment in which you receive a mild electric shock; you are in control of the level of shock that both you and your partner will receive; you set your partner's level very low even though it means your level of shock will be higher (and more painful).
30   Signing your favourite colour for a student who approaches you in a shopping mall and is working on a class project.
31   Changing a 20-cent piece for a stranger who approaches you.
32   You overhear one person giving another some directions; you realize the directions are incorrect, and you step over and correct him.
33   You agree to chaperone a small group of children from the juvenile detention centre on a trip to the zoo.
34   An appeal is made to you by a medical person to donate bone marrow for a seriously ill person (a stranger), and although it is a painful process, you agree.
35   Contributing time to read to a blind university student.
36   You work extra hard for your supervisor at work, knowing that s/he is eligible for a prize if productivity is up.
37   Turning the lights off on a parked car which has an open window (you don't know the owner).
38   Approaching a stranger lying on the street ahead of you, clutching his/her chest, to see what you can do.
39   A woman approaches you on the street and asks you to return some books to the library; although it is out of your way, you agree.
40   Breaking up a fight between two university students.
41   Giving money to a multiple sclerosis fund when a collector knocks on your door.
42   You give what change you have to a student who approaches you in a library asking for 50 cents to make some xerox copies.
43   While filling out a questionnaire for a market research organization you hear two children in the next room begin to fight; you go in to break up the fight because it sounds like one child is getting badly beaten.
44   Spending time with a mentally retarded boy.

---

* Denotes "new" episodes constructed for the study.

From the results of this preliminary investigation, a new sample was generated, consisting of the 25 helping episodes from the literature-derived list, three additional episodes which came from the original list of 62 and corresponded to three types of helping not covered by the 25, and 16 new episodes corresponding to the other neglected types of helping. This new sample may be said to "span" the popular typology of helping terms, in that there is at least one exemplar for every term. Having arrived at a representative sample of helping episodes, the next step was to see if the 16 new episodes (which represent forms of helping generally neglected in the helping literature) have any characteristics which distinguish them from those helping episodes more often studied by social psychologists.

Similarity ratings had already been collected for the original 25 and additional three from the first study, as explained in Chapter 2. Additional similarity ratings among the new 16 episodes, plus ratings for pairs from the new 16 and the old 28, were collected for this study in the same manner as before, with the same numbers of subjects involved. The combined matrix of similarity ratings was then input to a multidimensional scaling analysis of the total sample of 44 helping episodes.

Dimensional Interpretation of the Complete Sample Space

Inspection of the stress-values for the various MINISSA runs indicated that a four-dimension solution was the optimal. The stress level for four dimensions was 0.08 and adding further dimensions did not substantially improve the stress-level or interpretability. Figure 3.1 shows the configuration of points in the first three dimensions of the MDS space. The points representing members of the new 16 helping episodes are white; the rest are black. Casual inspection of the plots for this space revealed that many of the new helping episodes occupied an identifiable region in the space, indicating that perhaps they share properties in common which distinguish them from the old episodes. However, matters were complicated somewhat by the fact that a few old episodes were also in this region, while a few of the new episodes appeared to be lodged among the old episodes.

To find out what distinguished the new region from the old, a measure of connectivity with that region had to be devised. Initially, a measure was defined which indicated the ratio of connectivity between a given point and the set of points which definitely belonged to the new region, and the total connectivity of that point with all others in the space. Formally, this measure may be defined as:

$$C_j = \sum_{i \in R} s_{ij} / \sum_{i=1}^{N} s_{ij},$$

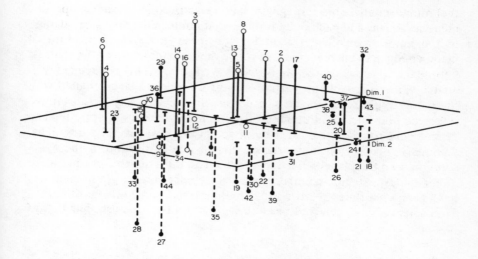

FIG. 3.1   New and old episodes in three-dimensional space.

where j indexes the point whose connectivity is being evaluated, i indexes all other points, $i\epsilon R$ refers to all points which are obviously members of R from among the new helping episodes, and s is the average similarity between the ith and jth points in the space. C_j should therefore be large for points which are in or close to the new region, since the sum of the s_{ij} for points in that region (the numerator term in the formula) will become large relative to the denominator. Thus, if we refer back to Figure 3.1, we should expect that C_{36} (for episode no. 36 in the space) will be large even though this episode comes from the literature-based sample, because it is lodged amongst the new episodes.

When this measure was computed for the 44 points, the values were then arranged in descending order and inspected for natural break-points to permit a more sensible assignment of points to the new region. On the basis of that inspection, 15 helping episodes were assigned to the new region, 8 to a "bridge" group and the remainder to the old region. A new measure of connectivity was then defined by:

$$C_j' = \frac{\sum\limits_{i\epsilon R} s_{ij} + \tfrac{1}{2}\sum\limits_{i\epsilon B} s_{ij}}{\sum\limits_{i=1}^{N} s_{ij}},$$

where $i\epsilon R$ again refers to points in the new region and $i\epsilon B$ refers to those in the bridge group. This measure is similar to the preceding one, save that the bridge connections are given half-weightings. The values for this measure assigned to each point became that point's "degree of belonging" to the new region. The reason for constructing a second measure of membership in the new region is to refine the representation of the contrast between the "new" and "old" types of episodes. This refinement will enable various scalable properties of those episodes to be correlated with the membership scale, to see whether any of them provide a substantive interpretation for the difference between these two types of episode. The groundwork for that analysis is discussed in the next several paragraphs. The reassigned region members are shown in a projection of the MDS solution onto the plane defined by the first and third dimensions, in Figure 3.2 below. New region members have been circled; bridge group members have been underlined. Notice the definiteness of the new region (the D1–D3 projection was selected because it provides the clearest view of this region).

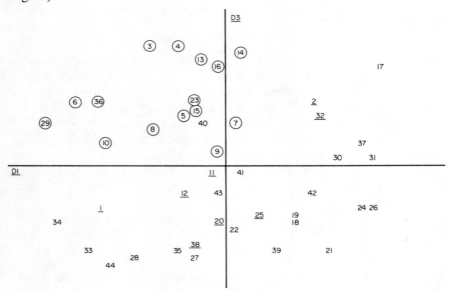

Fig. 3.2   The new region projected onto the D1–D3 plane.

Inspection of the various views of the space such as those provided in Figures 3.1 and 3.2 indicated that the points were arranged in a helical spiral, with an imaginary axis primarily aligned with the third dimension in the space. It was felt that this axis might be represented vectorially by the scale for membership in the new region defined above. The values for this scale were submitted as input for a PREFMAP analysis (Carroll, 1972). PREFMAP is an algorithm suited to assessing whether a scaled property can be represented as a vector in a Euclidean space of points possessing that property to varying degrees. In addition to finding the "best vector" and providing direction cosines to fix its orientation in the space, PREFMAP computes the correlation between projected values of each point on the vector and the data from the scale itself. This latter quantity is the best indicator of how adequate the vector representation is for the scale concerned. The vector representation for the new membership scale correlated with the original scale values at 0.84, indicating a good fit. As will be explained shortly, the vector aligned primarily with the third dimension, thus confirming the original intuition.

Bipolar trait ratings of the same kind used in the Chapter 2 study were obtained for the complete sample of 44 helping episodes, and were then used to interpret the four-dimensional MDS space. Table 3.3 contains the bipolar traits which PREFMAP results indicated were well represented as vectors in the space, along with their direction cosines and derived-vs.-original scale value correlations. For the sake of clarity, discussion of these vectors and their use in interpretation will be organized with respect to the three planes in the space defined by pairs of the first three dimensions.

TABLE 3.3 *Bipolar traits well-represented as vectors*

Trait names	Direction cosines by dimension			Derived scale-original scale correlations
	1	2	3	
Spontaneous/planned	−0.78	−0.15	−0.51	0.88
Informal/formal	−0.38	0.16	−0.90	0.81
Serious/not serious	0.32	−0.92	−0.11	0.73
Costs a lot/little	0.83	−0.09	0.42	0.74
Making feel good/ preventing feel bad	0.20	0.87	0.30	0.76
Helping improve/ preventing worsening	0.01	0.88	0.34	0.72
Friends only/ friends or strangers	0.77	0.56	−0.19	0.68
Intimate/non-intimate	0.58	0.17	−0.35	0.76
Personal/anonymous	0.65	0.43	−0.48	0.73
New membership scale	−0.50	−0.15	0.71	0.84

In the D1–D3 plane, three groups of vectors emerged:
1. new membership (versus old), and personal–anonymous;
2. costs a lot–costs little to help, and spontaneous–planned; and
3. Formal–informal.

None of these vectors projected much into the second dimension (D2), as their direction cosines in Table 3.3 show. Figure 3.3 displays the D1–D3 plane with these vectors projected onto it. On the basis of their near-orthogonality and high PREFMAP correlations, the bipolar trait "spontaneous-planned" and the vector for new membership were chosen as the best labels for the first and third dimensions, respectively.

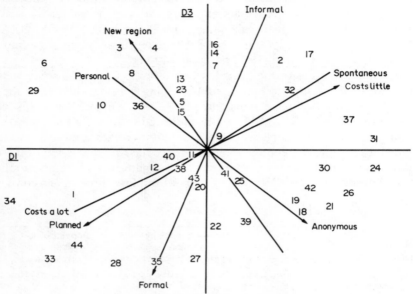

FIG. 3.3   Vectors in the D1–D3 plane.

In the D2–D3 plane, three bipolar traits were well aligned with the second dimension. These were "serious–not serious", "making people feel good–preventing people from feeling bad", and "making things improve–preventing things from worsening". These traits were of course highly intercorrelated. All PREFMAP correlations for the vector representations were approximately equal (0.73, 0.76 and 0.72, respectively), and so any of them could serve as reasonable labels for the second dimension. Figure 3.4 shows these vectors plotted into the D2–D3 plane, along with the new membership vector projection onto that plane. Notice that the new membership vector is nearly orthogonal to the others.

No important vectors projected into the D1–D2 plane which have not already been discussed, and so that plane will not be dealt with here. A summary of the dimension-labels is in order. These vectors are nearly orthogonal, with a maximum correlation among them of 0.32. Two of the three vectors which emerged in the Chapter 2 study have been reproduced by this study. The exception is the "giving–doing" dimension which, however, is an important variable in the original literature-derived sample.

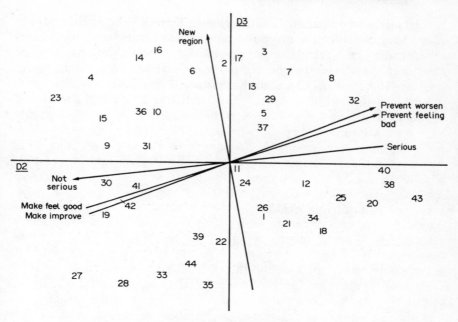

FIG. 3.4   Vectors in the D2–D3 plane.

Furthermore, the re-emergence of the "planned–spontaneous" dimension empirically confirms a theoretically based attempt at a typology of helping proposed by Benson *et al.* (1980).

The reader may be wondering by now whatever happened to the fourth dimension in the model. The answer is that no satisfactory interpretation was found for this dimension, although its presence in the model "cleaned up" the lower-order dimensions and made them more interpretable. This phenomenon in MDS analysis has been noticed by other investigators (e.g. Kruskal and Wish, 1978:58).

Distinctive Features of the Unstudied Region

Having successfully represented the new membership scale as a vector in MDS space, it remains to find some suitable interpretation for it. One obvious correspondence is the rather close alignment between the new membership and personal–anonymous vectors. The new episodes appear to be seen by subjects as predominantly personal forms of help, while most of the episodes from the literature are seen as anonymous. However, it would be helpful to have a more thorough-going interpretation, since the unstudied episodes may well be distinguished from their well-studied counterparts by more than one characteristic.

Interpretation of the unstudied region of helping episodes was accomplished in two ways. One was through regressing bipolar traits on the new membership scale defined in the preceding section of this chapter. The other technique was to represent the traits as contours in MDS space, checking them for overlap with the unstudied region. The bipolar traits consisted of those employed in the first study (see Chapter 2) and several new ones constituting the researchers' best guesses as to which properties would distinguish the old episodes from the new. There are several reasons for using more than one analytic technique here, and for selecting these two in particular. The fact that we have interval–level variables and we wish to use combinations of them to "account" for the new membership scale suggests a linear-model approach and, therefore, regression. However, the data-set is not sufficiently large, nor are the assumptions of multivariate normal distributions and homogeneity of variance sufficiently satisfied, to warrant relying totally on a regression approach. More fundamentally, there is no *a priori* reason to suppose that a linear combination of variables will do the trick. Therefore, a technique which contrasts with the regression model is required to supplement this analysis, preferably one that does not involve a linear model or the assumptions underlying the regression approach. As will become evident later on, the contour-map approach fits the requirement nicely. If both approaches yield similar interpretations of the distinction between the new and old episodes, then we should be justified in having some confidence in the robustness of that interpretation.

Stepwise regression procedures were used to obtain the best set of bipolar scales to "account" for the new membership scale. The model which emerged as most reasonable consisted of four such variables which together accounted for 68 percent of the variance in new membership scale values. The bipolar traits, along with their beta-weights and contributions to explained variance, are presented below in Table 3.4.

TABLE 3.4   *Regression on the new membership scale*

Scale-trait	Beta	R^2 change	Simple R
Personal/Anonymous help	−0.33	0.51	−0.71
Helping because asked/ Helping because feel like	0.39	0.06	0.44
Friends only/Fr. or stranger	−0.37	0.06	−0.53
Don't know what to do/ Know what to do	−0.23	0.05	−0.33

Notice that by far the greatest proportion of explained variance is contributed by the "personal–anonymous" scale. It is the best single explanatory trait for the new membership scale. Other traits which correlated highly with the scale, but which were excluded from the final model because they were overridden by other traits in the regression procedures, included "non-intimate–intimate" ($r = 0.60$), "responding to request–responding to own judgement" ($r = 0.41$), "self initiated–other initiated" ($r = 0.41$), and "informal–formal" ($r = -0.40$).

As a final check on the adequacy of the regression model, values from the regression equation were input to PREFMAP, to see whether a vector similar to that for the new membership scale would emerge. The direction cosines of the regression vector were quite similar to those for the new membership scale vector, and the correlation between the derived and original regression-equation values was 0.77, indicating that this regression model stood up as a vectorial dimension for the MDS space, in addition to capturing the essence of the new region.

The regression characterization of the distinctions between the new and old helping episodes provides a situational frame with four parameters defining the situational differences:

1. the perceived affective quality of help being given (personal vs. anonymous);
2. the motivational basis for helping (internal vs. external);
3. the prior relationship between helper and helpee (whether friends or not); and
4. the cognitive familiarity of the helper with the situation.

The neglected types of helping may then be characterized as:

1. personal (and intimate);
2. internally motivated (one feels like helping; self-initiated);
3. occurring between friends only; and
4. cognitively unfamiliar (uncertain as to what to do).

While some studies of helping behaviour have used helping situations which possess one or another of these traits, very few have employed situations which have all of them in combination.

Some of the bipolar traits which were related to the new membership scale could not be represented as vectors in MDS space. Sometimes this was due to the fact that the traits tended to "clump up" in specific regions of the space, rather than being smoothly graded from one end of the space to its opposite end. Even so, in several such cases, the traits obviously have a coherent representability as a region in the space that cannot be captured by a vectoral approach. These traits therefore require methods other than regression for determining whether they help distinguish the new helping episodes from the old. Figure 3.5 displays three such traits, represented in terms of dot-size. Each dot represents an episode, and the size of the dot indicates the extent to which that episode was perceived as occurring only between friends, personal, or intimate. These traits were rated on a 7-point scale, and the sub-ranges on that scale for each size of dot are shown in the figure. As can be seen in Figure 3.5, the new region roughly corresponds to the upper-left quadrant of the D1–D3 plane. It is evident that most of the

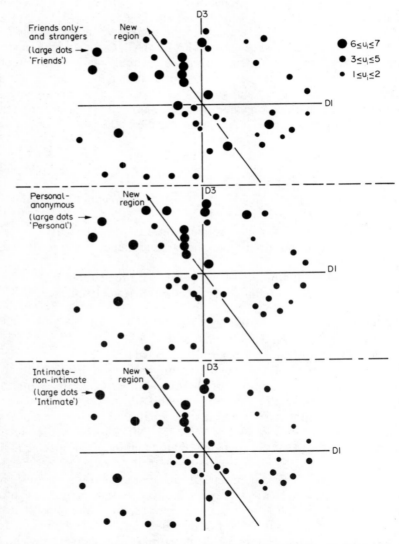

Fig. 3.5   Extent of intimacy, personalness, and friend-exclusiveness of episodes.

new region episodes are seen as intimate, personal and occurring only between friends.

Another group of bipolar scales referred to subjects' attributions of external or internal motivation for helping. As Figure 3.6 shows, the new region contains relatively few good examples of other-initiated help. Correspondingly, subjects tend to see requested help as lying outside the unstudied region. Requested help tends to occur in the non-serious situation where the helper is trying to improve things or make people feel good.

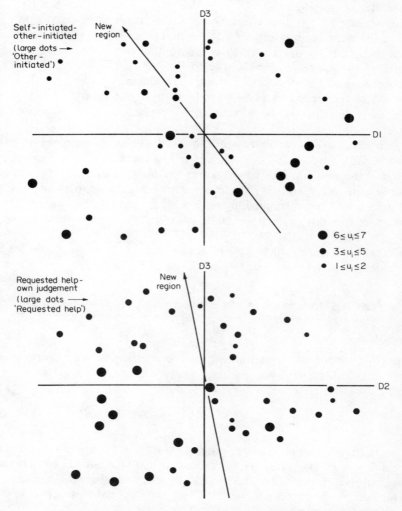

FIG. 3.6   Extent of other-initiation and perceived requestedness of episodes.

In summary, the regional interpretation of the unstudied region yields the following distinguishing features:

1. the unstudied region contains helping episodes which tend to be perceived as personal, intimate kinds of helping which occur only between friends; and

2. most other-initiated or requested help lies outside the unstudied region.

Notice that this second statement does not imply that only other-initiated helping has been studied by social psychologists; obviously many studies of self-initiated helping exist.

How adequate is this characterization of the unstudied region? For the most part, it has replicated the major features of the regression approach, but we have yet to compare the two approaches for their explanatory power. A simple way to do this is to combine the various bipolar scales in set-theoretic fashion to produce a composite scale whose properties reflect the two conditions set out in the preceding paragraph. We may do this by borrowing the fuzzy-set notions of union and intersection.

According to standard fuzzy-set theory, the union of fuzzy sets A and B gives a set whose membership values follow the rule that membership in $A \cup B$ is the maximum of membership values in A and B. The fuzzy-set intersection of A and B gives a set whose membership values are the minimum of the membership values in A and B. Letting u denote membership value, in mathematical notation, the above rules imply that $u_{A \cup B} = \max(u_A, u_B)$ and $u_{A \cap B} = \min(u_A, u_B)$.

In the case with which we are concerned, we require a rule for the membership values in a set defined by

$$((\text{personal}) \cup (\text{intimate}) \cup (\text{friends only})) \cap ((\text{self-initiated}) \cup (\text{unrequested})).$$

Applying the rules for determining the membership values of fuzzy unions and intersections, we obtain a new scale which is defined as:

$$u_{\text{new}} = \min(\max(u_p, u_i, u_f), \max(u_s, u_r)).$$

If we then compute eta-squared when u_{new} is the independent variable and the new membership scale is the dependent variable, we get 69 percent of the variance explained, which agrees quite closely with the amount explained by the regression model. Thus, both approaches have about the same explanatory power.

Discussion and Conclusions

It makes sense to conclude this study by returning to the starting-point, namely the question of how social psychological studies have been distributed over the different varieties of helping. From the same bibliography used to extract the original list of helping situations used in Chapter 2, a random sample of 123 references was taken and coded for their location in the MDS space. Because of the moderate sample size, there were many zeros in the space (types of helping to which no member of the sample corresponded) and so correlations are probably somewhat misleading. Nevertheless, it is worth noting that the new membership scale and the personal–anonymous scale emerged as by far the best correlates with the number of studies done of various kinds ($r = -0.44$ and -0.45, respectively).

A projection of the distribution of studies onto the D1–D3 plane of the MDS space is shown in Figure 3.7. From this figure it is also apparent that planned and high-cost forms of help (as contrasted with spontaneous and low-cost) have been somewhat neglected in the social psychological literature as well. This pattern agrees with the findings in a literature search by Benson *et al.* (1980). The major exception is helping episode no. 34, with eight cases, which corresponds to several studies using blood donation as the situation. The graphic display obviously confirms the claim that there is a nearly unresearched region of helping with the characteristics described in this chapter. The single exception, with seven cases in the upper middle region, corresponds to studies of children's sharing behaviour. No studies of adults' sharing behaviour were found in the sample.

The MDS space, and the sample and dimensional model underlying it, have several other uses which will be explored in subsequent chapters. One of the most important for cognitive studies is the construction of attitude-scale or questionnaire items on helping whose meanings are empirically grounded. The resources for this application derive from the ratings obtained for the helping forms in the sample on their degree of fit with the terms taken from the dictionary. Given a complete set of such ratings for any lexical term over the sample of 44 helping forms, a researcher who wishes to use that term in a questionnaire could ascertain its fuzzy-set location as a series of contours in the MDS space.

A full set of ratings for the lexical-term list would provide the basis for an empirically grounded taxonomy of helping terms, which could supplant recent intuitive attempts at such taxonomies. The method for constructing this taxonomy consists of straightforward applications of fuzzy-set theory and descriptive statistics. Both of these uses for the space and lexical-term list will be presented in Chapter 5.

The MDS model may be of use to researchers and theorists of helping

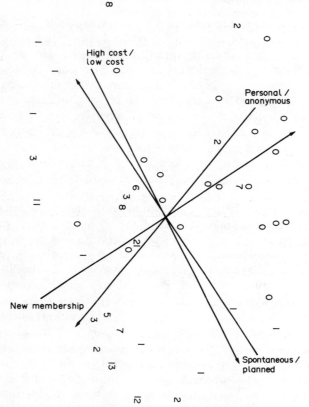

Fɪɢ. 3.7   Distribution of social studies in the episode space.

behaviour in three ways. First, because it is based on a more complete sample of helping than that employed in the Chapter 2 study, it indicates to researchers what types of helping need studying most urgently. It seems unlikely that an adequate theoretical understanding of helping can emerge in social psychology if an entire domain of helping episodes remains largely unstudied. Intimacy has occasionally been discussed in the helping literature (Staub, 1978: chapter 9). However, we do not recommend that researchers simply fill in the blank regions of the space with results from more isolated empirical investigations, nor do we feel they should necessarily use our exemplars in the neglected region for research purposes. What is needed instead is the study of helping episodes which are varied systematically along the various dimensions, in such a way as to minimize or control for all other differences among the episodes. This is similar to the procedure recommended by Staub (1978, pp. 121–124) who advocates the scaling of helping situations along certain dimensions. Only through this use of a model such as ours can the helping research field move closer to a genuine theoretical overview.

A second use for the present classification scheme derives from the fact that it is both empirical and cognitive, characteristics which, in conjunction, have been missing from other classification attempts. If the dimensions located in this study actually represent salient distinguishing features of helping for ordinary people, then it is likely that social norms and behaviours may be at least partly explained by reference to these dimensions. It is expected that such explanations will not be simple correlational statements, but instead complex contingencies involving different regions of the space.

One area in which the present model may prove useful is in the search for personal variables relevant to helping. Some approaches, such as that of Pomazal and Jaccard (1976), imply that an individual's beliefs, values, motivations and normative expectations about certain types of helping can be strong predictors of helping behaviour, but only when the type of helping is narrowly specified (e.g. donating blood). This contrasts with other investigators (Rushton, 1980; Staub, 1978) who have argued for personality traits which predict helping behaviour across wide varieties of situations.

The present model suggests a middle-range approach, one which recognizes that personal characteristics (such as personal norms, prosocial values and personality traits) may predict behaviour in certain regions of the multidimensional space but not in others. Some results from Benson *et al.* (1980) suggest that personality traits predict helping behaviour to a greater degree in planned than in spontaneous helping situations. Another related possibility is that there are different "helping personalities" which make people more likely to help in certain kinds of situations than others. For instance, some people may be eager to help family and friends in personal or intimate situations, but not to provide assistance to strangers. Likewise, others may be quite helpful in everyday matters and yet feel it is best not to become involved in emergency situations; and still others may be constantly involved in planned and formal types of helping to the exclusion of other varieties.

This line of thought is consistent with past research which indicates that behavioural consistency is found only across very similar situations (Mischel, 1968). Bar-Tal (1976) claims that emergency and non-emergency situations arouse different social norms, motives and hence response-sets (p. 51). Staub (1978) argues that an individual's prosocial orientations may operate only within restricted ranges of situations (p. 47), and that accurate predictions of helping may not be possible without an understanding of the connections between personal characteristics and the salient features of situations. If the cognitively based taxonomy presented in this chapter has isolated salient dimensions by which individuals classify helping situations, then it should aid in finding the ranges within which people's prosocial concerns are likely to operate. This possibility is explored further in Chapter 7.

A third way in which the present model may assist theorizing is by specifying the situational parameters within which the predictions of an entire theory might be expected to hold true. For instance, an equity-theoretic view of helping may hold for non-serious forms of help, but not for emergency situations where other norms and motives may override those connected with equity. Likewise, it is difficult to see how equity concerns would be relevant to people engaging in anonymous helping with complete strangers, whom they are unlikely to see again. Further, equity considerations may also be less relevant in the very personal types of helping. Rubin (1973) indicates that people in close relationships often do not expect reciprocation for positive acts because what benefits one person benefits the other as well. Thus, equity-theoretic predictions may hold only for the middle range of the personal–anonymous dimension. This issue is further discussed in Chapter 7.

Of more immediate importance, however, is the stability and generalizability of the MDS space. Are there important differences in the overall perception of helping between professional helpers and laypeople? What about intercultural differences? Do men and women perceive helping differently? These and related questions are taken up in the next chapter.

4

A Multisample Study of the Cognitive Taxonomy of Helping

M. SMITHSON and P. R. AMATO

Method

IN THIS chapter, an assessment is made of the generalizability of the cognitive taxonomic model proposed in Chapter 3. This assessment is based on a study of five samples, ranging from university students to non-student community members and helping professionals. The Chapter 3 model, although interesting and intuitively reasonable, was based solely on a rather small sample of university students. A natural question is which features of that model are generalizable, and whether there are interpretable differences among various populations in their perceptions of helping episodes.

The comparison of complex cognitive structures is not easily achieved. Obviously, the approach adopted here must focus on a multidimensional scaling technique. But despite the recent availability of methods and computer programs for comparative multidimensional scaling analyses (for early efforts, see Wexler and Romney, 1972 and Wish, Deutsch and Biener, 1972; for more recent work see Forgas, 1980, Coxon and Jones, 1978, Carroll, Pruzansky and Kruskal, 1980, and Borg and Lingoes, 1980), actual attempts to make such comparisons in detail are relatively rare and the methods for doing so are as yet unstandardized. Therefore, the first section of this chapter is devoted to describing our approach in some detail.

Subjects and Procedures

Five samples were obtained for this study. The subjects performed similarity judgement tasks on pairs of helping episodes, and bipolar construct rating tasks identical to those involved in the Chapters 2 and 3 studies. Since the objective here was to determine whether the Chapter 3 results are generalizable, the sample of 44 helping episodes from that study were used, as were the following bipolar constructs: spontaneous–planned, informal–formal, serious–non-serious, know what to do–don't know, personal–anonymous, costs a lot to help–costs little, giving what I have–doing what I can, passive–active, and help given to friends only–given to friends or strangers. The similarity-judgement matrices and bipolar construct rating scales were broken up into 12 sections of manageable size (approximately 260 judgements per subject) to avoid fatigue or boredom. Every rating was performed by six to ten subjects per sample.

The samples are briefly described below:

1. Thirty-nine students in the Behavioural Science Department at James Cook University who had indicated an intention of pursuing either clinical psychology or social work studies (hereafter referred to as the "student helper" sample).
2. Twenty-eight Behavioural Science students who were majoring in a non-helping-oriented field (research psychology, sociology, anthropology, or other fields in the humanities and natural sciences) or who had not indicated a clear preference for a major (henceforth referred to as the "student non-helper" sample).
3. Thirty-one individuals from the Townsville community who were not university students and who did not work in a help-giving profession (henceforth referred to as the "community" sample).
4. Eighty first-year psychology students at the American River College in California (hereafter referred to as the "American student" sample).
5. Seventy-six nurses and nursing students at the Townsville General Hospital (henceforth referred to as the "nurses" sample).

These groups were chosen as a result of a compromise between the original study design and the practical problems which arose in attempts to implement that design. The initial intent was to balance the samples in a 2×2 design with the two control factors being education (university vs. non-university) and involvement in a helping profession. The first three and the fifth samples correspond roughly to such a design, with the two Behavioural Science groups representing the university helper and non-helper half, and the nurses and community samples representing the non-university half. These groups obviously may differ in ways other than their educational level and (non)involvement in professional helping. The American student sample was obtained as a result of an opportunity to collect data from another country.

Logic and Method of the Analysis

This section focuses on the sequential logic of the analytic techniques employed for comparing the five samples. Given the dimensional nature of the Chapter 3 model, two possible sources of intergroup differences in perception were deemed relevant: (1) people from different populations might use different constructs with which to organize their own taxonomies of helping; and (2) people might perceive the same constructs in different ways when applying them to helping episodes. That is, one group might use the serious–not serious construct as an organizing principle, while this construct might be absent from the taxonomies of another group. Or on the other hand, one group might give an average rating of high personal cost for an episode which another group tended to rate low in cost.

These two types of differences may be cross-classified to provide four broad classes of intergroup cognitive differences: (1) the groups agree on both the constructs they use for organizing helping episodes and their perceptions of those constructs; (2) the groups use the same constructs, but perceive them differently; (3) the groups use different organizing constructs, but perceive the same constructs in similar ways; and (4) The groups use different organizing constructs and also differ in their perceptions of the same constructs. This list is not meant to be definitive; many mixed or ambiguous situations could arise. However, this classification is convenient because it exposes the major possibilities to which any analytical approach in this type of study must be sensitive.

Because the available options in multidimensional scaling analysis for group comparisons all require that the groups perceive dimensional constructs in highly similar fashion (cf. Carroll and Chang, 1970), the first priority should be an investigation of the degree to which subjects from the different samples perceive constructs similarly. The next section of this chapter is devoted to such an inquiry, which was carried out along two lines. The first was an assessment of the extent to which subjects were using the constructs as continuous variables as opposed to discrete (and dichotomous) categories. An attempt was also made to locate any intergroup differences in this tendency. The rationale for exploring this question first is that the systematic comparison of group differences on continuous variables requires different statistical techniques from those suited for the exploration of such differences on categorical variables.

The second line of inquiry consisted of a correlational analysis of the intergroup differences in the bipolar construct ratings, and a comparison of the interrelationships among the constructs. The first comparison was accomplished by correlating the mean group ratings on each helping episode for each construct, across helping episodes and for all sample pairs. Sample differences were then dissected in terms of intergroup differences in ratings on specific episodes. The second comparison, concerning the relationships among the constructs, involved an investigation of between-group similarity in correlations between pairs of constructs. The objective here was to determine whether pairs of constructs which were perceived as unrelated by one sample would also be seen as unrelated (hence uncorrelated) by another sample. This comparison was accomplished first by normalizing the interconstruct correlations via the usual transformation (cf. Blalock, 1979:419) and then correlating the transformed correlations across all pairs of constructs, for every pair of samples.

The results of the intergroup comparisons on the constructs informed the second stage of the analysis, which involved comparing the actual cognitive organization of helping episodes for the five samples. There are several possible techniques for such a comparison, and in the multidimensional scaling literature the options fall into three camps. First, there is the simple but somewhat draconian approach of performing separate MDS analyses on each sample, and then comparing the results in a rather qualitative fashion (see Forgas, 1976 for an example). A more sophisticated approach is to use one of the so-called three-mode techniques of factor analysis or multidimensional scaling (cf. Carroll and Chang, 1970; Tucker and Messick, 1963) which permit groups to be treated as subjects and include various quantitative summaries of group or individual differences. These methods, however, require that all subjects use the same constructs for organizing helping episodes, and that they perceive those constructs in rather similar ways. Finally, recent developments in "confirmatory" factor analysis and multidimensional scaling (e.g. Carroll, Pruzansky and Kruskal, 1980 or Borg and Lingoes, 1980) allow the researcher to assess the fit between any set of similarity judgements and a predetermined configuration by constraining the possible range of MDS solutions for representing the new data in Euclidean space.

The third option was rejected at the outset for two reasons. First, the only candidate for an *a priori* configuration was the model generated in the Chapter 3 study. But there were no persuasive reasons for believing this model to be an appropriate basis for comparing the five samples. Furthermore, it was not feasible to construct the rigorous side-constraints needed for confirmatory analysis. It was felt that confirmatory analysis might find better use in studies of intergroup or intercultural differences in the perception of helping subsequent to this one, particularly if such studies employ random sampling.

As will become apparent in the section to follow, the construct comparisons among groups indicated that a three-mode approach might yield meaningful results. The technique selected was the INDSCAL method as developed by Carroll and Chang (1970) and implemented in the MDS(X) program series (Carroll and Chang, 1977). The INDSCAL solution, while fitting all five samples reasonably well and replicating the major features of the Chapter 3 model, nevertheless suffered several defects which indicated that it might be inadequate as a general model. Consequently, separate MDS runs were conducted for the five samples, and detailed comparisons were made between the resulting configurations. The MINISSA program from the MDS(X) package was employed for this purpose.

Exploring the Bipolar Constructs

Continuous Variables or Discrete Categories?

Before attempting to assess various groups' perceptual similarities regarding the rating of helping episodes on bipolar constructs, it is reasonable to ask whether the subjects are treating those constructs as continuous variables or dichotomous categories, or indeed what the underlying distributions of ratings look like. This question has substantive implications as well as statistical relevance, which is one of the reasons for dwelling on it here.

As a first step, simple histograms of the frequencies for each sample's ratings on every bipolar construct were examined for evidence of skewness and coverage of the range. As may be recalled from Chapters 2 and 3, the scales had 7-point ranges. All but two of the constructs exhibited coverage of the range and symmetry for all five of the samples. The two exceptions were Costs and Knowledge constructs (cost a lost–costs little to help, and know what to do–don't know what to do), both of which were skewed and showed limited coverage of the scale range. It was decided to exclude these two constructs from the correlational analysis because of their low variability in the five samples. Evidently most subjects find most kinds of helping relatively low in cost and believe that they would know what to do in many situations requiring help. A percentage distribution of frequencies for the five combined samples on each construct is shown in Figure 4.1.

The graphs in Figure 4.1 provide a qualitative indication of whether the subjects generally treat these constructs as continuous variables or not. The evidence seems inconclusive, insofar as there is a tendency for frequencies to bunch up at the ends of the distributions, but the middle-range values are certainly not unused. What is needed here is an assessment of the "relative variation" exhibited here in subjects' ratings, a measure which contrasts the sample variation with the maximum possible variation (which would occur, of course, when all ratings were at either extreme of the scale range).

Such measures have in fact been proposed from a variety of sources, such as information theory (cf. Arbib, 1964; Theil, 1967), the study of social inequality (Taagepera and Ray, 1977; Allison, 1978) and fuzzy-set theory (De Luca and Termini, 1972; Knopfmacher, 1975; Loo, 1977). The measure adopted here follows the work of Smithson (1979, 1981) and satisfies several criteria for such measures:

$$T2 = 1 - \left[\left(\sum_{i=1}^{N} u_i^2 - N\bar{u}^2 \right) \Big/ \left(\sum_{i=1}^{N} Q_i^2 - N\bar{Q}^2 \right) \right]^{\frac{1}{2}},$$

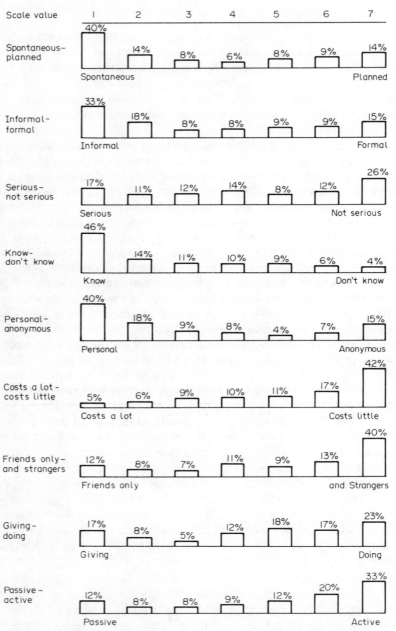

FIG. 4.1 Percentage distribution for five samples of ratings on bipolar constructs.

where N is the number of ratings in the sample, and the Q_i are equal to either 0 or 1, such that the mean of the Q_i is approximately equal to the mean of the ratings (denoted by $\bar{u}$).

$T2$ has a number of properties which make it preferable to other measures for the sort of analysis to be conducted here (see Smithson, 1981 for a comparative discussion). The denominator of the right-hand term is the maximal possible variation in the ratings, given the mean and sample size. Thus, the denominator normalizes the numerator so that the right-hand term varies from 0 to 1, achieving maximum value when the ratings are all equal to either 0 or 1. To make this a measure of the "fuzziness" of a construct, it suffices to subtract this term from 1, which mean that $T2$ may be interpreted as a proportional deviate away from 1. $T2$ therefore permits a sensible assessment of the degree to which subjects use the constructs in a continuous or a categorical fashion, with a high value indicating fuzziness and a low value indicating a dichotomy.

Table 4.1 displays the $T2$ values for each of the five samples' ratings on each of the bipolar constructs. With the possible exception of the Cost construct, the values point to a moderate tendency for subjects in all samples to see helping episodes in categorical terms, although it is evident that their ratings are by no means entirely categorical. Another striking pattern in this table is the high agreement among samples, with the slight exception of the nurses who appear to treat the constructs somewhat more categorically than the other groups. The results overall indicate that, while the constructs are being treated as continuous for the sample of helping episodes provided, there is a tendency for subjects to dichotomize them.

TABLE 4.1   T2 *values for five samples' ratings on all bipolar constructs*

Construct	Australian non-help students	Australia helping students	Australian community	Nurses	U.S.A. students
Spontaneous/Planned	0.27	0.27	0.28	0.21	0.29
Formal/Informal	0.32	0.32	0.29	0.21	0.30
Serious/Not serious	0.34	0.34	0.33	0.30	0.35
Know/Don't know	0.40	0.43	0.47	0.29	0.45
Personal/Anonymous	0.29	0.28	0.27	0.25	0.26
Costs little/A lot	0.32	0.37	0.37	0.33	0.35
Friends only/& Strangers	0.32	0.34	0.31	0.24	0.32
Giving/Doing	0.35	0.36	—	0.23	0.32
Active/Passive	0.34	0.35	—	0.25	0.36

One possible explanation for the results thus far is that the sample itself is not fine-graded enough. It would be reasonable to ask whether other samples of helping episodes would yield similar results. To assess this possibility, data were collected from the nurses and social work students in which they were asked to perform the same rating-tasks as had been done for the sample of 44 helping episodes, but on helping episodes that they had been involved in. Nurses and social-work students who had recently participated in placements in professional agencies were asked to recall and rate nine helping episodes which they had undergone during their previous week's work. The social-work students were also asked, at a later time, to perform the same task for six examples of helping which they could recall having engaged in, outside of work, during the preceding week.

Comparisons of $T2$ values between these samples of helping and the nurses' and social-work students' ratings for the 44 hypothetical episodes yielded equivocal results. The nurses were somewhat more categorical about their work experiences than about the hypothetical episodes, but the reverse was true for the social workers. Thus, it is probably a reasonable conclusion that the preceding analysis was not affected by an artefact of sampling.

Sample Differences in Construct Perception

Given the fact that the ratings data are a mixed set of dependent and independent observations, from multiple raters, none of the usual straight-forward statistical tests for differences among groups (e.g. ANOVA or MANOVA) are appropriate; nor is there any guarantee that they would yield meaningful results, given the large number of comparisons which would have to be made. A compromise between the need for meaningful summary statistics and the requirements of a rigorous analysis of group differences was produced in a correlational approach.

All pairs of samples were compared on each construct by correlating the mean ratings (averaged over the subjects in the sample) for each helping episode on that construct. Table 4.2 below shows the correlations between group pairs, arranged by construct. The Cost and Knowledge constructs have been excluded from this part of the analysis, because of their skewness and low variability. Root-mean-square values are reported at the bottom of each sub-table.

Overall, there is a strong correlation between pairs of groups in their perceptions of constructs. The major exception is the nurses' group, which appeared to perceive the active–passive construct differently from the other subject samples. More will be said of this difference shortly. For the most part, the samples exhibit correlations in the mid-0.7 to 0.8 range, indicating that the subjects in those groups are using the constructs in similar ways.

Another important difference to examine is the relationships among the constructs themselves, as evidenced by their correlations with one another. Interconstruct correlations of mean ratings within each sample were computed, and normalized via the conventional transformation for correla-

TABLE 4.2   *Intersample correlations of mean ratings on all bipolar constructs*

Spontaneous/planned

	Australian helping students	Australian non-help students	Australian community	U.S.A. students	Nurses
Australian helping students	—				
Australian non-help students	0.91	—			
Australian community	0.87	0.83	—		
U.S.A. students	0.86	0.82	0.88	—	
Nurses	0.83	0.81	0.70	0.76	—
	Root-mean-square $R = 0.83$				

Informal/formal

	Australian helping students	Australian non-help students	Australian community	U.S.A. students	Nurses
Australian helping students	—				
Australian non-help students	0.73	—			
Australian community	0.60	0.61	—		
U.S.A. students	0.70	0.73	0.81	—	
Nurses	0.72	0.58	0.70	0.71	—
	Root-mean-square $R = 0.69$				

Serious/not serious

	Australian helping students	Australian non-help students	Australian community	U.S.A. students	Nurses
Australian helping students	—				
Australian non-help students	0.91	—			
Australian community	0.87	0.81	—		
U.S.A. students	0.81	0.84	0.74	—	
Nurses	0.88	0.83	0.85	0.75	—
	Root-mean-square $R = 0.83$				

Personal/anonymous

	Australian helping students	Australian non-help students	Australian community	U.S.A. students	Nurses
Australian helping students	—				
Australian non-help students	0.83	—			
Australian community	0.72	0.74	—		
U.S.A. students	0.71	0.74	0.61	—	
Nurses	0.75	0.68	0.53	0.79	—
	Root-mean-square $R = 0.72$				

TABLE 4.2   *(Cont.)*

Friends only/& strangers

	Australian helping students	Australian non-help students	Australian community	U.S.A. students	Nurses
Australian helping students	—				
Australian non-help students	0.88	—			
Australian community	0.88	0.84	—		
U.S.A. students	0.83	0.77	0.82	—	
Nurses	0.79	0.78	0.78	0.78	—
Root-mean-square $R = 0.82$					

Giving/doing

	Australian helping students	Australian non-help students	U.S.A. students	Nurses
Australian helping students	—			
Australian non-help students	0.69	—		
U.S.A. students	0.77	0.74	—	
Nurses	0.68	0.69	0.62	—
Root-mean-square $R = 0.70$				

Active/passive

	Australian helping students	Australian non-help students	U.S.A. students	Nurses
Australian helping students	—			
Australian non-help students	0.70	—		
U.S.A. students	0.75	0.85	—	
Nurses	0.45	0.51	0.52	—
Root-mean-square $R = 0.65$				

tions (Blalock, 1979:419). These normalized correlations were then correlated for all pairs of groups, to assess intergroup differences in the relative orientation of the constructs. The goal here was to assess whether the various groups of subjects relate the constructs to one another in similar ways, prior to deciding among various MDS options for comparing their cognitive helping taxonomies.

Table 4.3 shows the intergroup correlations, and the root-mean-square value at the bottom of the table. Obviously, there is at least as strong an agreement among samples concerning the relative orientation of the constructs to one another as the agreement on the actual ratings themselves. Again, the nurses differ more than any of the other samples, except when compared with the community sample. It is interesting to note that the American student sample agrees highly with the other student samples and reasonably well with the community sample also.

TABLE 4.3   *Correlations of intra-group, inter-scale correlations for five samples*

	Australian helping students	Australian non-help students	Australian community	U.S.A. students	Nurses
Australian helping students	—				
Australian non-help students	0.84	—			
Australian community	0.88	0.88	—		
U.S.A. students	0.82	0.89	0.79	—	
Nurses	0.77	0.72	0.90	0.62	—
	Root-mean-square $R = 0.82$				

The major difference in construct perception which requires interpretation is the nurses' difference from the other samples on the active–passive construct. One route to an interpretation is by examining the correlations between the nurses' ratings on the Activity construct and their ratings on others. Inspection of these correlations reveals that the Activity construct does not correlate with the serious–not serious or the giving–doing constructs (correlations are 0.09 and 0.16, respectively). This pattern differs from all four other groups, in which the ratings for the Activity construct correlated moderately strongly with both the Seriousness and giving–doing constructs (root-mean-square correlations are 0.46 and 0.59, respectively). In short, for the nurses, active helping is not seen to be "doing" type in "serious" situations, as is frequently the case for the other groups.

Thus far, all evidence points to the conclusion that, with the occasional exception of the nurses' group, the subjects in the populations sampled for this study use the constructs in rather similar ways. Thus, if the groups differ in the actual organization of helping episodes in their respective cognitive taxonomies, the reason for such differences will likely be that they are using different constructs as organizing principles, rather than using the same constructs in different ways.

Given that the groups are similar in their perceptions of the constructs tested, the decision of whether to use a three-mode multidimensional scaling technique (as opposed to a separate MDS run for each group) depends on whether the groups are likely to share a group of constructs as common organizing principles in their taxonomies of helping episodes. This is the central concern of this chapter. The only *a priori* evidence which has direct bearing on this question was the extent to which the groups made similar similiarity ratings about pairs of helping episodes. Table 4.4 below shows the intergroup correlations for mean similarity ratings across all pairs of helping episodes. Since these correlations are moderately strong and positive, a three-mode approach is likely to yield meaningful results. The next section deals with the use of such an approach in analysing group differences and in constructing a general taxonomic model of helping.

TABLE 4.4   *Correlations of similarity ratings for five samples*

	Australian helping students	Australian non-help students	Australian community	U.S.A. students	Nurses
Australian helping students	—				
Australian non-help students	0.60	—			
Australian community	0.52	0.42	—		
U.S.A. students	0.58	0.51	0.51	—	
Nurses	0.50	0.48	0.43	0.52	—

Root-mean-square $R = 0.51$

Five Sample Three-Mode Multidimensional Scaling Analysis

Method and Analytical Techniques

The three-mode multidimensional scaling technique used in this study involved two algorithms which will be briefly explained here. The first, and the actual model on which the three-mode MDS in this study was based, is known as the Individual Differences Scaling model (INDSCAL, the main reference for which is found in Carroll and Chang, 1970). INDSCAL performs a multidimensional scaling analysis of a three-way set of (dis)similarity matrices, with the usual assumptions involved in ordinary (two-way) MDS, and an additional two assumptions about the subjects' cognitive schema and the rotatability of the dimensions derived in the INDSCAL solution. The first assumption is that the subjects all organize the stimuli (in this study, of course, the helping episodes) via a shared set of dimensional constructs. The subjects may weight these dimensions differently in their own organization of the stimuli, but they must use all of them to some extent. The second assumption is that the axes or dimensions produced in the INDSCAL solution may not be rotated to a more "meaningful" position, as is the case with ordinary factor analysis and multidimensional scaling. This means that the axes produced by IND-SCAL are unique in their orientation, and therefore must be labelled or interpreted in that orientation and no other. This restriction might seem overly confining, but the second analytical technique used in this study provides a way of overcoming it to some degree.

   An INDSCAL analysis produces two spaces rather than just one. The first is the "group space", similar to the conventional MDS output in which the episodes are located in a finite Euclidean space with respect to the orienting dimensions. The second space, called the "subject space", locates the subjects themselves in the same Euclidean space, representing each subject as a point. The coordinates for the subject correspond to the numerical weights inherently assigned by that subject to each dimension; these weights are the INDSCAL estimates of the salience or importance of each dimension to the subject. Additionally, the square of the distance from the origin in the space to the subject point is proportional to the amount of variance in that subject's data which is accounted for by the INDSCAL solution. The further away from the origin the subject point is, the better the fit between the INDSCAL solution and that subject's (dis)similarity judgements. Further information on INDSCAL and its uses may be obtained from several sources, but one of the most readable introductions is in Kruskal and Wish (1978).

The second algorithm employed is known as the Preference Mapping (PREFMAP) technique (Carroll, 1972). Originally developed for the analysis of individual differences in preference, certain special cases of this technique also have uses in determining the extent to which a construct can be represented in vectorial or ideal-point form in MDS space.

There are two kinds of representation we shall be concerned with here. The first of these, the so-called vector model, represents a given construct as a directed line pointing through the space. Perpendicular lines taken from each episode-point in the space to the vector determine that point's rating on the vectorial representation of the construct. The correlation between these "derived" ratings and the real ratings of the episodes on the construct is an indication of the fit between the vectorial representation and the construct being represented. Thus, there are two important kinds of information in this analysis: the correlation between the derived and actual construct ratings, and the direction-cosines which indicate the orientation of the vectorial representation with respect to the dimensions in the space. Given a vector whose derived–actual ratings correlation is high, it may be used an an interpretive label for a dimension in the space if the angle between the vector and that dimension is sufficiently small.

The second representation corresponds to the so-called unfolding model as first generalized to the multidimensional case by Bennett and Hays (1960). In this model, each construct is represented as an "ideal point" in the space, with episode-points' distances from the construct-point defining the derived rating of the episode on the construct. Again, the correlation between derived ratings and the actual construct ratings determines the extent to which the construct has been successfully represented by this model (hereafter referred to as the "distance model", in accordance with more recent terminology). This model is not useful for labelling dimensions, but it can aid greatly in relating individual constructs to the group space produced by the INDSCAL analysis.

The sequence of analysis employed was quite straightforward. First, the INDSCAL analysis was performed using the groups as "subjects", and thereby locating each sample in the subject space. Once the resulting solution has been evaluated for stability and its dimensionality decided upon, the PREFMAP analysis was used for mapping constructs into the space.

The INDSCAL Analysis

The INDSCAL runs, using several random starting configurations as required by the program, yielded a stable solution in which only a few individual points showed any tendency to wander. Further, in all runs, the percentages of explained variance (which indicate the extent to which the solution faithfully recovers the similarity information in the raw data) were virtually identical. Therefore, it is probably a safe conclusion that the resulting space is not the product of a degenerate solution from the program.

Solutions were obtained with dimensionality ranging from 1 to 5. The percentages of variance explained in the different dimensionalities were 15, 26, 35, 40 and 44, in order of ascending dimensionality. Since the options selected for the INDSCAL runs required that each dimension be extracted separately, these increasing percentages may be interpreted directly in terms of the percent of variance explained added by each new dimension. Thus, the first dimension contributed 15 percent, the second 11 percent, the third 9 percent, the fourth 5 percent and the fifth 4 percent. Obviously, the first three dimensions are of approximately equal importance, while the latter two do not contribute much individually.

The subject space revealed few differences among the groups in terms of their dimension weightings, and in their degree of fit with the solution. The figure of 44 percent explained variance implies a correlation of about 0.66 between the INDSCAL-derived similarities and the original data. When the groups' data were correlated with their derived similarities (taking into account not only the INDSCAL spatial configuration but also the groups' own dimensional weights), the correlation values ranged from 0.63 to 0.70, indicating very similar degrees of fit.

The overall fit between the solution and the original data is not outstanding, as indicated by the fact that five dimensions are required to recover 44 percent of the variance. This result indicates that, especially given some of the preceding indications of differences between the nurses and the other groups, separate MDS runs on each might be warranted. However, the degree of fit is not trivial either, and merits further exploration into the interpretability of the space.

Interpretation of the INDSCAL Solution

The interpretation of the INDSCAL space has two objectives. The first is to attach meaning to the dimensions and their orientations. The second, of course, is to determine the extent to which this space replicates the major features of the taxonomy proposed in Chapter 3. In summary, these features are reviewed here. First, there was a distinct region occupied primarily by episodes corresponding to types of helping neglected in the social psychological literature. The space itself was a four-dimensional solution, with three of the dimensions clearly labelled by the spontaneous–planned, serious–not serious and personal–anonymous constructs. The giving–doing construct had been important in the Chapter 2 study but had not re-emerged as a vector in the Chapter 3 taxonomy.

The INDSCAL space was inspected for evidence of a region similar to that found in the Chapter 3 study, distinguishing the unstudied episodes from those taken out of the social psychological literature. Such a region was found, showing up plainly in the plane defined by the first and second dimensions, and even more so in the first and fifth dimensional plane. This latter plane is displayed in Figure 4.2, with the "neglected" episodes circled. Only two of these were lodged among the well-studied episodes; these two were also rather marginal members of the region in the Chapter 3 results. In general, this aspect of the original study appears replicated in the INDSCAL space.

PREFMAP runs were performed on the bipolar constructs, using both the vector and the distance models. The first and second dimensions were convincingly labelled by the spontaneous–planned and serious–not serious constructs, respectively. Several other constructs were well represented as vectors in the space. However, the third, fourth and fifth dimensions did not yield interpretations, either through labelling from the constructs or intuition.

There are two possible explanations for the uninterpretable higher-order dimensions. One is that the INDSCAL solution simply has not captured the various groups' perceptions of helping episodes clearly enough because of nonshared constructs underlying the groups' taxonomic schema. The other possibility is that there is at least one shared underlying construct which has not been found in the studies to date. This second explanation cannot be discounted, since all groups' weightings for the higher-order dimensions are approximately equal, thus indicating that no minority of groups is using those dimensions exclusively. Furthermore, in both the Chapter 2 and 3 studies, an unexplained higher-order dimension emerged which, although not crucial for interpretability of the space, was useful in "cleaning up" the lower-order dimensions.

In summary, although it replicated several of the main features of the Chapter 3 taxonomic model, the INDSCAL space is unsatisfactory as a

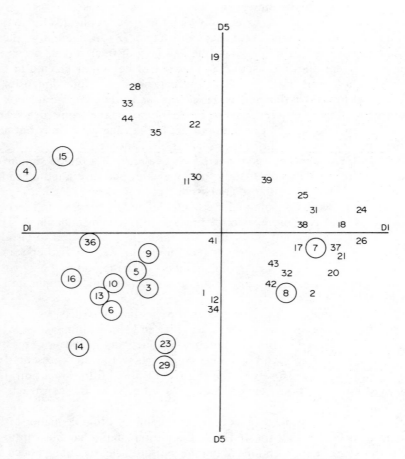

Fig. 4.2   The new region in the INDSCAL space, D1–D5 plane.

final generalized model. The percentage of explained variance is not exceptionally high, three of the five dimensions are uninterpretable at present, and the relationships among the bipolar constructs are not faithfully reproduced when they are mapped into the space (personal–anonymous has a lower average correlation with the planned–spontaneous construct than its position in the space would indicate). For these reasons, the messier but perhaps more meaningful tasks of separate MDS analyses for the five samples was undertaken, to further explore the generalizability of the taxonomic model and the differences between groups.

Separate MDS Analyses for the Five Samples

Features of the MDS Spaces

The stress-values obtained for dimensionalities from 1 to 5 are shown in Table 4.5, for each of the samples' MDS solutions. Inspection of this table clearly shows that the samples are similar in the dimensionality of the spaces representing their taxonomic schema. In all cases the preferred dimensionality is either 3 or 4.

TABLE 4.5   *Stress-values[1] for MINISSA runs on five samples*

Sample	Dimensionality				
	1	2	3	4	5
Australian helping students	0.48	0.29	0.20	0.16	0.13
Australian non-help students	0.47	0.30	0.22	0.17	0.14
Australian community	0.48	0.31	0.23	0.19	0.16
U.S.A. students	0.49	0.32	0.23	0.18	0.15
Nurses	0.49	0.32	0.23	0.18	0.15

[1] Stress-Dhat used for measuring goodness-of-fit.

All samples' MDS spaces (the four-dimensional solutions) were examined for evidence of the region distinguishing the unstudied helping episodes from their well-studied counterparts. In all samples but the Community group, this region emerged clearly (that is, with three or fewer "misclassifications"). The Community sample's region was not as distinct, with two unstudied episodes lodged among the well-studied and four well-studied episodes in the unstudied region (or a total of six misclassifications). The evidence, therefore, generally confirms the existence of a neglected region of helping akin to that described in Chapter 3. The case for the importance of this region would be strengthened, of course, by demonstrating that this "neglected" type of helping occurs frequently in everyday life. Chapter 6 presents some data testing this proposition.

PREFMAP runs were performed for each sample's construct data, in an attempt to assess the representability of the constructs in the MDS spaces and also to interpret the dimensions. Table 4.6 displays the derived–actual ratings correlations for the vector model. The correlations are generally somewhat lower than they were for the INDSCAL analysis because the combined samples' ratings were used for the INDSCAL run, which resulted in better reliabilities and therefore enhanced vectorial representability.

The spontaneous–planned construct is reasonably well represented as a vector in all samples, while serious–not serious and personal–anonymous are well represented in four out of five cases. Giving–doing and active–passive are well represented except for the nurses, who appear to have more complex representations of these concepts. Neither of these constructs

TABLE 4.6 *Correlations of derived and actual bipolar scale ratings for the vector model*

	Australian helping students	Australian non-help students	Australian community	U.S.A. students	nurses
Spontaneous/Planned	0.78	0.71	0.79	0.76	0.72
Formal/Informal	0.70	0.55	0.60	0.67	0.58
Serious/Non-serious	0.73	0.62	0.69	0.85	0.60
Know/Don't know	0.45	0.33	0.43	0.68	0.33
Personal/Anonymous	0.65	0.68	0.68	0.72	0.72
Costs little/A lot	0.51	0.63	0.36	0.51	0.49
Friends only/& Strangers	0.74	0.69	0.61	0.57	0.46
Giving/Doing	0.73	0.69	—	0.73	0.51
Passive/Active	0.79	0.80	—	0.70	0.18

improved in their representability when the distance model was used, although both serious–not serious and personal–anonymous did in the cases where they were not well represented by the vector model.

The final step in this analysis was to find appropriate labels for dimensions (or at least planes in the spaces). Table 4.7 summarizes the results of the labelling, with constructs listed along with the dimensions with which they were aligned. The four constructs which emerged as important in the Chapters 2 and 3 studies dominate the labels, with only two out of 18 coming from the other constructs. Spontaneous–planned is a clear label for all five samples, while personal–anonymous clearly emerges in four, serious–not serious in three, and giving–doing in three of the four cases for which data are available. Also noteworthy is the fact that in almost every case there is one dimension for which no construct stands as a label or onto whose planes no construct projects substantially. The nurses' sample involves two uninterpreted dimensions. The existence of one uninterpreted dimension in all cases underscores the proposal that there is a major construct, possibly generalizable, which has not been found by the present research.

The present analysis suggests that the main features of the taxonomic model proposed in Chapter 3 may generalize to a reasonably wide variety of people in English-speaking countries. Specifically, the current model indicated by the results involves four constructs (spontaneous–planned, serious–not serious, personal–anonymous and giving–doing) and a clear distinction between an unstudied type of helping best described as "personal" help which occurs mainly between friends.

Other Sample Splits: Age, Sex and Political Affiliation

In addition to the notion that professional helpers might perceive helping differently from lay people, it has also been suggested that women may

TABLE 4.7   *Dimensional labels for the five samples*

Sample	Dimensions	Constructs
Australian helping students	1	Friends only–& Strangers
	2	Serious–Not serious, Active–Passive
	1 & 2	Giving–Doing
	1 & 4	Spontaneous–Planned
Australian non-help students	1	Giving–Doing
	2	Personal–Anonymous
	3	Spontaneous–Planned
Australian community	1	Spontaneous–Planned
	2	Serious–Not serious
	1 & 3	Personal–Anonymous
U.S.A. students	1	Serious–Not serious, Giving–Doing
	2 & 3	Personal–Anonymous
	1 & 3	Spontaneous–Planned
Nurses	1	Spontaneous–Planned
	1 & 4	Personal–Anonymous

differ from men, the young from the old, and conservatives from liberals in their perceptions of helping (e.g. Gaertner, 1973; Hoffman, 1977). The five samples of data analysed in this study provided an opportunity to tentatively explore some of these propositions, albeit under imperfect sampling conditions. As a result, the two student and community samples were combined and redivided into men and women, under-25 and older age-groups, and finally those professing an affiliation with the Labour party and those affiliated with the Liberals (this latter split required the exclusion of those indicating no party preference or a third party affiliation, which resulted in samples of 41 Labourites and 27 Liberals).

These pairs of groups were then compared in much the same way as the five samples were in the preceding sections, but without the use of a three-mode technique. First, the bipolar construct ratings were correlated for each pair, resulting in a root-mean-square correlation of 0.80 for the age-groups, 0.81 for the sex-groups and 0.73 for the political groups. The correlations for the age and sex groups were all quite strong, indicating that in these samples the young and old, and men and women, do not differ much in their perception of the constructs. This conclusion was further strengthened by the fact that the correlations of transformed interconstruct correlations between group-pairs were also quite high, with the age-groups producing a value of 0.89, the sex-groups 0.92, and the political parties 0.88. All of these values are higher than most of the corresponding values for correlations between pairs among the five samples (see Table 4.3).

The MDS runs performed for each of these groups generally confirmed the overall similarity between the sexes and the young and old. The correlations between the similarity-judgement data for the group-pairs yielded values of 0.70 for the age-groups, 0.65 for the sexes and 0.58 for the political groups, all three of which exceed the root-mean-square of 0.51 for the corresponding five-sample correlations. Table 4.8 shows the stress-levels for MDS solutions of varying dimensionality for each pair of groups, indicating that in all cases the preferred dimensionalities of their spaces are very similar.

TABLE 4.8   *Stress-values[1] for MINISSA runs on sample splits*

	Dimensionality				
Sample	1	2	3	4	5
Young	0.49	0.30	0.21	0.17	0.14
Old	0.46	0.29	0.20	0.16	0.13
Male	0.45	0.29	0.20	0.16	0.14
Female	0.48	0.30	0.21	0.17	0.14
Liberal	0.46	0.28	0.20	0.16	0.13
Labour	0.47	0.30	0.20	0.16	0.13

[1] Stress-Dhat used for measuring goodness-of-fit.

The outstanding difference which emerged in this exploration was between the political groups. As mentioned before, their root-mean-square correlation for their construct ratings was 0.73, which is somewhat lower than the other two group-pair averages of 0.80 and 0.81. The reason for the depressed value is that the correlation between the two groups was 0.64 for the active–passive construct and only 0.55 for the giving–doing construct. These two were the only correlations below the average of 0.73. It should be noted that the Australian Labour and Liberal parties are known for their differences in approaches to matters of welfare and social assistance generally (cf. Graycar, 1979). However, most writings on such differences have treated them solely in terms of values differences or conflicts of interest. The interesting finding here is that Labourites and Liberals may differ in their perception of helping, with regard to the donation and intervention aspects. An interpretation of this difference might therefore suggest future avenues for research into the political ideology of helping.

A comparison of the correlations among construct-pairs for Labour and Liberal subjects revealed that the Active–Passive construct is related to the Cost construct in the Liberal sample ($r = 0.47$), but not in the Labour sample ($r = 0.05$). In other words, there is a moderate tendency for Liberals to associate active helping with high personal cost, although this association does not obtain in the Labour sample. One possible explanation is that the two groups perceive the Cost construct differently as well. However, the mean ratings for the Cost construct were nearly equal for the two samples, and the correlation between their ratings was 0.70, indicating a reasonably strong agreement on the assessment of personal cost.

Intriguingly enough, a similar relationship did not emerge in the Liberal sample between the Cost construct and giving–doing. But this may be due to a tendency for the Liberals to rate all forms of helping somewhat higher on the "doing" end of the scale than the Labourites. The Labour mean rating was 4.24 (on a scale with a range from 1 to 7) with a standard error of 0.21, while the Liberal mean was 4.97 (more toward the "doing" end of the scale) with a standard error of 0.24. Thus, the two means differ by about 3.3 standard errors (this yields a t-statistic value of 2.32, which at 86 df has a significance level of about 0.02, for those who believe in significance-testing on non-random samples). This difference seems to indicate that Liberals see nearly all forms of helping in terms of intervention rather than donation. The mean ratings for individual episodes in the Liberal sample fell into the "giving" half of the scale only 6 times (out of 44 episodes), as compared to 17 times for the Labourites.

The Liberals differed the most from the Labourites on their rating of helping episodes which fall into the general class of donating-type help (examples include letting an acquaintance borrow a book, bringing a gift to a nephew, sharing food, donating bone marrow for an operation, and giving money to the Multiple Sclerosis Fund). These results, exploratory though they be, suggest that the differences between left-wing and right-wing attitudes about social welfare may include more than values disagreements or conflicts of interest. Conservatives may well perceive welfare functions differently than progressives, insofar as they see most helping in terms of intervention. It is even possible that the much-vaunted notion that Conservatives are chary of welfare spending stems from this perceptual difference, since our results also suggest that Conservatives see intervention as costly. The political ideology of helping has seldom been studied from a cognitive standpoint, but such research could extend understanding in this area if the results of this exploration are any indication.

Generalizability of the Present Taxonomy

To close this chapter, we return to the issue of the taxonomic model and its generalizability. As proposed at the end of the five-sample study, several features of the model presented in Chapters 2 and 3 seem to have been replicated. Subjects in all the samples differentiate clearly between the kinds of helping typically studied by social psychologists and another kind which has been neglected. The properties of this neglected type of helping have been investigated in Chapter 3, but its dominant characteristic seems to be that it is a personal sort of helping which usually occurs between friends. The question of how important this type of helping is in everyday life (and, therefore, its relative importance for social psychological research) is taken up in Chapter 6.

Four constructs appear to dominate people's cognitive schema for organizing helping episodes: spontaneous–planned, serious–not serious, personal–anonymous and giving–doing. These constructs are not entirely unrelated to one another, but in no case are strongly related. Table 4.9 shows the root-mean-square interconstruct correlations, averaged across the five samples. Since these correlations were quite similar in all five samples, the values in the table are stable indications of the extent to which these constructs are related. For research purposes, we recommend treating them as separate and independent, since they are in fact nearly orthogonal. Chapter 6 presents a number of studies assessing the usefulness of these constructs in providing an overview of people's norms and behaviours in helping situations.

TABLE 4.9   *Root mean-square interconstruct correlations*

	Spontaneous	Informal	Serious	Know	Personal	Cost	Friends	Give–Do	Passive
Spontaneous	—								
Informal	0.72	—							
Serious	−0.10	−0.30	—						
Know	0.25	0.23	−0.29	—					
Personal	−0.36	−0.12	0.12	0.10	—				
Cost	−0.54	−0.53	0.25	−0.40	0.15	—			
Friends	−0.46	−0.12	−0.23	−0.23	0.55	0.39	—		
Give–Do	−0.29	−0.14	−0.35	0.26	0.16	0.14	0.39	—	
Passive	0.16	0.23	−0.39	0.15	−0.06	−0.31	0.20	0.56	—

The above-mentioned constructs may not be the only generalizable organizing principles used by people in their cognitive schema; nor are the labels used in this study the only possible ones for the constructs that have been discovered. Future research will tell whether these constructs are the only ones and which labels are the most appropriate. There is surely a need for extensive investigation into attitudes and perceptions about helping. Chapter 5 presents some suggestions and illustrations for methods which might be used in such research. The issue of categorical labels for types of helping is also pursued in Chapter 5, with a reanalysis of some data from the Chapter 3 study using fuzzy-set methods to explore the structure of the English lexicon of helping terms.

5

Cognitive Representations of Helping

M. SMITHSON

Extending the MDS Model

THE MODEL of cognitive schema developed in Chapters 3 and 4 provides a four-dimensional organizing principle for people's views of helping. Although this model appears to have reasonable generalizability, we do not regard it as final; nor do we believe multidimensional scaling is the only method for modelling cognitive schema. In this chapter we will present an analysis of the lexical category data from the Chapter 3 study, as a demonstration of how this data may be combined with the MDS approach for an exploration into two types of application:

Type I: Using the fuzzy membership ratings for the lexical categories to represent each categorical term as a set of contours in the MDS space. This representation tells investigators what regions of the space are covered by the term, and thereby allows them to construct questionnaire or attitude-scale items using the term with some knowledge of what the term "means" in the context of the MDS model. It also enables researches to select terms for such items in such a way as to deliberately refer to only certain types of helping. And finally, this information can be used to select or construct helping situations which correspond to an individual term and no other, for use in empirical studies.

Type II: Enhancing the capacity of the MDS model to represent cognitive schema. The available information may be used to construct an empirically based typology of helping terms which corresponds to the cognitive schema of subjects. This taxonomy may then inform the researcher of important regions and clusters within the MDS space itself. This kind of analysis may be carried out either at the group or individual level, so that either group or individual schema are represented.

Both types of applications have implications for theory construction and research in the helping field, and also for clinical and practical uses. These implications will be discussed briefly at the end of the chapter, and then further expanded in Chapter 7. This chapter is organized in two major parts. The first deals with fuzzy-set representations of lexical terms for helping and the Type I applications listed above. The second part entails the development of a taxonomy of helping categories and its use in extending the MDS model.

Constructing Fuzzy-Set Representations of Helping Terms

As indicated in Chapter 3, ratings were obtained from 35 subjects on the degree of belonging of each helping form in every category in the lexical list of terms. These ratings were taken on a scale from 0 to 10, with intermediate values assigned via the hedged phrases presented in Chapter 3, 0 indicating that the item did not belong at all to the category, and 10 indicating full membership of the item in the category. In this chapter, for the sake of consistency with conventional work on fuzzy sets, we shall use a scale which goes from 0 to 1 rather than from 0 to 10, and membership values will be denoted by the letter u. As demonstrated in Chapter 3, fuzzy-set membership can be mapped into the MDS space as a series of contours, to represent the regions of the space covered by the set itself. This representation may then be used in a variety of ways.

An example of such a representation is given in Figure 5.1. The lexical category "saving" is displayed as contours in the D1–D2 plane. The numbers in the map are the membership values which indicate the extent to which subjects perceive each episode to be an exemplar of "saving", with higher numbers representing better examples of "saving". A boundary-line has been drawn around the best exemplars, which occur at the "serious" end of the second dimension, as might be intuitively expected. Another boundary indicates the region of the poorest examples, which are clumped at the opposite end of dimension 2. A researcher interested in using this term in a questionnaire or attitude-scale item could use this information to ascertain exactly what traits the term would call up in the minds of respondents.

The potential for improving attitude or value surveys regarding helping is considerable. The literature presently includes a variety of scales and inventories purporting to measure various prosocial attitudes or values, such as altruism (Wrightsman, 1964), empathy (Mehrabian and Epstein, 1972), or social responsibility (Berkowitz and Lutterman, 1968). Virtually all of these measures use the lexicon of helping terms unsystematically, usually including overly broad terms (e.g. "helping", "aiding", or "assisting") or narrow terms of dubious connection with the concept being measured. If one were to construct, say, a values inventory focusing on helping, contour representations could be used to aid the researcher in choosing terms which referred selectively to different types of helping, and in ensuring that the sample of terms adequately covered the entire helping space.

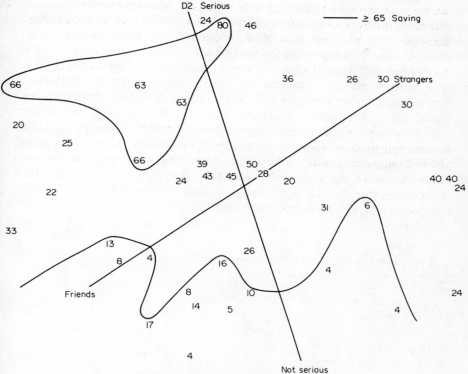

FIG. 5.1   Contour map of "Saving" in the D1–D2 plane.

In cases where the researcher wishes to use responses to situations which exemplify a helping concept (as in Wrightsman's illustration of altruistic behaviour via the example of stopping to assist a person whose car was disabled), ratings for the degree of membership of each situation in the concept-term could be obtained to ensure that the situations were in fact exemplars of the concept. Finally, in cases where a broad concept is being investigated, the researcher can locate situational exemplars in the MDS space itself, using information on their spatial locations to determine whether an adequately varied sample of exemplars has been provided. Returning to the "saving" concept displayed in Figure 5.1, for instance, exemplars of this term spread widely across the first dimension (spontaneous-planned). If we wanted to tap attitudes about saving-type help, it might be wise to use both planned and spontaneous kinds of episodes. The two examplars of "saving" which are furthest apart include donating bone marrow for a seriously ill person, and coming to the aid of a heart-attack victim, which are in some respects radically different situations.

The researcher can also check the meaning of composite terms, or of terms connected by conjunctives such as "and", "or", or "but not". Again, borrowing from standard fuzzy-set theory, the membership values for items in a union of fuzzy sets is simply the maximum membership value of each item in all the sets being combined. Thus, for instance, the membership values for the union of "rescuing", "saving", and "intervening" are equal to max (u_{res}, u_{sav}, u_{int}). Figure 5.2 shows the contour map for this union of three terms, projected again onto the D1–D2 plane. Notice that the picture is rather similar in general to Figure 5.1. The same kinds of representations can be provided for terms connected by "or" (using the minimum of membership values rather than the maximum), or even for terms connected by combinations of conjunctives.

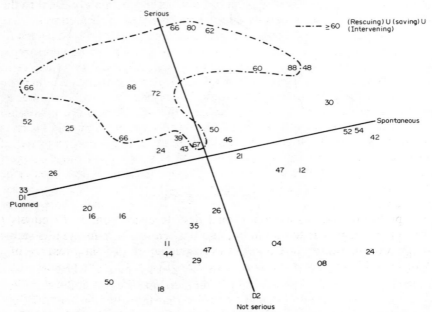

Fig. 5.2   Contour map of the union of "Rescuing", "Saving" and "Intervening" in the D1–D2 plane.

Researchers may also wish to know how fuzzy their categorical terms are over the sample of stimuli. Some terms may have very definite, "crisp" categorical boundaries while others may have graded or blurred edges. To some extent, this information can be determined by inspecting the distribution of membership values for the category concerned. If the values are always close to 0 or to 1, then the category is fairly "hard-edged", but if there are many intermediate values then the category is fuzzy. For some application it may be useful to have a summary measure of fuzziness with which to compare categories. This is especially true where a researcher wants to choose between two nearly synonymous terms on the basis of their relative fuzziness. A number of measures have been proposed (e.g. De Luca and Termini, 1972, Knopfmacher, 1975; Loo, 1977), but most of them have stability problems. The measure recommended here is one adopted by Smithson (1981, 1982) which was introduced in Chapter 4:

$$T2 = 1 - \left[\left(\sum_{i=1}^{N} u_i^2 - N\bar{u}^2 \right) \bigg/ \left(\sum_{i=1}^{N} Q_i^2 - N\bar{Q}^2 \right) \right]^{\frac{1}{2}},$$

where N denotes the number of stimuli in the sample, and the Q_i are equal to either 0 or 1, such that the mean of the Q_i is approximately equal to the mean of the u_i. The u_i denotes the membership of the ith stimulus. As noted in Chapter 4, the denominator of the right-hand term normalizes $T2$ by the maximal possible variability in the u_i given their mean and sample size (maximum variability occurs when the u are all equal to 0 or 1, or in other words when the category is non-fuzzy). The right-hand term may be taken to be a coefficient or relative variation among the u_i (relative, that is, to the maximal possible variation among the u_i). Now, since maximum variability occurs when the u_i are all equal to 0 or 1, the right-hand term is actually negatively associated with fuzziness. To make a measure of fuzziness out of this term, all we need do is subtract it from its largest possible value, which is 1. Thus, as the u_i are closer to 0 and 1 (extreme values), the right-hand term approaches 1, and the value of $T2$ approaches 0, indicating that the category is not very fuzzy. $T2$ may therefore be interpreted directly as a proportional deviate away from 1. $T2$ equals 1 when the category is totally fuzzy, and 0 when it is non-fuzzy; it is stable under varying sample size and not overly influenced by the presence of a lot of 0-valued items in the sample (see Smithson, 1982 for proofs).

As an example, consider Figure 5.3 below, in which the contour map in D1–D2 for the term "freeing" is shown, and compare it with the map for "saving" in Figure 5.1. Note how the exemplars for "freeing" are more sharply differentiated from the other items in the space than they are in the "saving" map. The value of $T2$ for "freeing" is 0.37, while for "saving" $T2 = 0.58$, so "freeing" is less fuzzy.

An additional useful application for measures of fuzziness is to find out whether modifiers of categorical terms make them fuzzier. From the psychology of judgement literature we know that modifiers such as "very" or "extremely" are likely to render a given category more discriminable to human judges. It also turns out that these intensifiers make categories less fuzzy (e.g. Smithson, 1982) and of course reduce their coverage of the stimuli being classified (cf. Kochen and Badre; 1974, MacVicar-Whelan,

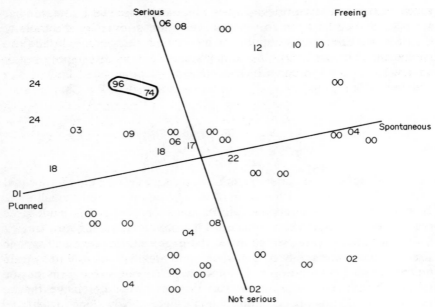

FIG. 5.3   Contour map of "Freeing" in the D1–D2 plane.

1974; Hersch and Caramazza, 1976). Researchers using such modifiers as "somewhat" or "not very" may find that the resulting modified categories are fuzzier and broader (cf. Smithson, 1982).

Fuzzy-set methods also permit researchers to establish the degree to which two terms are synonymous, at least with respect to a finite collection of stimuli. This is done by using a measure of intercategory overlap (cf. Smithson, 1981) which behaves somewhat like the ordinary correlation coefficient. Imagine a two-way data set consisting of membership values u_{ij} for M stimuli and N categories, with i indexing the stimuli and j indexing the categories. Bezdek (1974) showed that

$$\sum_{i=1}^{M} u_{ij}\, u_{ik}$$

is proportional to the amount of membership "shared" by the categories j and k. What is being measured here is the amount of intersection between the two categories. The product of u_{ij} and u_{ik} has been proposed as a measure of intersection for several set-theoretic reasons, some of which make intuitive sense. For instance, it seems reasonable that the amount of intersection should never exceed the smaller of the two membership values, and $u_{ij}u_{ik}$ satisfies this condition. Likewise, intersection should reach its maximum (say, 1) only when both u_{ij} and u_{ij} equal 1, and this is so for $u_{ij}u_{ik}$. To convert this to a normed measure of overlap, it suffices to divide it by the amounts of membership carried, on average, by the two categories. The result is an overlap coefficient whose appearance is somewhat similar to a correlation coefficient:

$$Mjk = \frac{\sum\limits_{i=1}^{M} u_{ij}u_{ik}}{\left(\sum\limits_{i=1}^{M} u_{ij}^2 \ \sum\limits_{i=1}^{M} u_{ik}^2\right)^{\frac{1}{2}}}.$$

Despite the apparent similarity with Pearson's r, however, Mjk is not based on the covariance term, which measures covariation away from the means for the two variables concerned. Instead, Mjk measures the extent to which the membership values for the two categories deviate similarly away from 0, relative to the amount of membership carried by each. Thus, it is a measure of relative scale-equivalence rather than covariation (for further explanations and details, see Smithson, 1981 and 1982). Mjk varies from 0 to 1, equalling 1 if the two categories are synonymous in the sense of having the same relative amounts of membership for each stimulus in the sample. Thus, for instance, the terms "comforting" and "consoling" were found to be highly synonymous over the 44 stimuli in the sample of helping forms used in this study, attaining an Mjk value of 0.97.

Establishing synonymy, however, is not by itself sufficient to guarantee the interchangeability of two terms. It is quite possible for one term to be a "special case" of the other. Fortunately, standard fuzzy-set concepts lead to easily employed measures for fuzzy-set inclusion. In ordinary set theory, set A includes set B if all elements in set B are also in A. In fuzzy-set theory, fuzzy-set A is said to include fuzzy-set B if each element is at least as strong a member of A as it is of B. In membership values terms, this amounts to saying that $u_B \leq u_A$. An easy way to see whether this is the case to produce a bivariate plot of the membership values for the two categories. For instance, a plot of the membership values for the terms "assisting" and "succouring" would reveal clearly that the former is a special case or subcategory of the latter, since all points in such a plot would fall below the diagonal running from the origin to (1,1).

However, the inclusiveness of one category over another may not always be that obvious. For this reason, it would be useful to have a measure of the degree of inclusion between two categories (cf. Kempton, 1978, for some examples of data where such a measure is sorely needed). Several candidates for inclusion coefficients have been proposed, but the one adopted here is defined by:

$$Ikj = \frac{\displaystyle\sum_{i=1}^{M} \max (0, u_{ij} - u_{ik})}{\displaystyle\sum_{i=1}^{M} | u_{ij} - u_{ik} |} \; .$$

The interpretation of I_{kj} is straightforward. If category k includes category j, then we should expect that, for the majority of stimuli, $u_{ij} \geq u_{ik}$, by virtue of the inclusion rule discussed in the preceding paragraph. Therefore, $u_{ij} - u_{ik}$ ought to be positive. In ambiguous cases, $u_{ij} - u_{ik}$ might be negative or zero for some i. One way of measuring the preponderance (or lack) of positive values is to sum them and then divide them by the sum of the absolute values of all the $u_{ij} - u_{ik}$. If all the $u_{ij} - u_{ik}$ are positive, then this ratio will be equal to 1, and if none are positive, then it will be 0. If we apply this formula to the membership data for "assisting" and "succouring", we get a value of 0.99, indicating nearly perfect inclusion. The main properties of this coefficient are:

1. $Ikj = 0$ iff $u_{ij} \leq u_{ik}$ for all i, which means category j includes category k;
2. $Ikj = 1$ iff $u_{ij} \geq u_{ik}$ for all i, which means category k includes category j;
3. $Ikj = 1$ by definition if $u_{ij} = u_{ik}$ for all i; and
4. $Ikj = 1 - Ijk$, which means the measure is symmetrical (except when $u_{ij} = u_{ik}$ for all i).

The applications for Ikj and Mjk in combination are numerous. Some of their possibilities will be shown in the next section of this chapter. With them, a researcher may document whether a pair of terms is truly interchangeable, or whether one is a subset of the other, or whether they are synonymous in any sense. For instance, not only are "assisting" and "succouring" related by the fact that the former includes the latter, but they are also reasonably synonymous, having a value for Mjk of 0.91. The terms "succouring" and "ministering to", on the other hand, are highly synonymous with a Mjk value of 0.92, but non-inclusive, since for them $Ikj = 0.41$.

A Taxonomy of Helping Categories

The overlap coefficients defined in the preceding section provide a similarity measure for any pair of categorical terms. Thus, it should be possible to use a matrix of such coefficients as the input for a clustering routine, as a first step in generating a taxonomy of the terms. Various schemes for fuzzy clustering have been proposed (cf. Ruspini, 1969, and Bezdek, 1974). Here, we follow the work of Johnson (1967) by using his hierarchical clustering method (in the MDS(X) program series), specifically the so-called "diameter" method. The reason for this is that in fuzzy-clustering methods, the input data usually consist of similarities between items which are themselves elements and not categories as such. Here, the similarities are between categories which are themselves fuzzy sets. Thus, at the level of individual set members, even non-fuzzy clusters may be ultimately treated as fuzzy, since they are clusters of fuzzy categories.

The data for this taxonomic study were collected from 32 university student volunteers, and consisted of membership ratings for 40 helping categories from the lexical list over all 44 helping forms in the sample defined in Chapter 3. Table 5.1 contains the list of these categories, with an indexing number which will reference each category for the remainder of this chapter.

TABLE 5.1   *List of helping categories*

Index category		Index category		Index category	
01	Assisting	14	Taking care of	28	Collaborating with
02	Donating	15	Intervening	29	Succouring
03	Protecting	16	Showing kindness	30	Encouraging
04	Rescuing	17	Aiding	31	Educating
05	Sharing	18	Enabling	32	Defending
06	Lending a hand	19	Giving handouts	33	Fixing
07	Saving	20	Benefiting	34	Shielding from
08	Being charitable	21	Being generous	35	Nursing
09	Co-operating	22	Freeing	36	Reinforcing
10	Empathizing	23	Ministering to	37	Consoling
11	Giving	24	Inspiring	38	Forewarning
12	Solving	25	Comforting	39	Exonerating
13	Altruistic	26	Giving information	40	Nurturing
		27	Healing		

Figure 5.4 displays the diameter method solution (see Appendix 2 for the overlap coefficient matrix). The "cluster diameter" figures at the side of the diagram refer to the lowest similarity rating between a word-pair in clusters which have been formed up to that level. There is a natural cutoff point at the 0.83 level, and another at the 0.72 level. In the absence of any other information, the usual interpretive treatment of this kind of clustering is to choose a cutoff point, and then label the clusters which have been formed up to that level. It is generally assumed that the weaker the connection in a cluster (that is, the greater the diameter), the more general the level. This links the concept of taxonomic hierarchy with degree of similarity. But if we make that assumption, then a cluster such as 13–17 ("altruistic" and "aiding") is held to be less general than 23–29 ("minister-

ing to" and "succouring"). These latter two categories are in fact much more specific than the former pair, so this interpretation makes little sense. However, we have yet to utilize the other source of information at hand, namely the extent to which various categories include others.

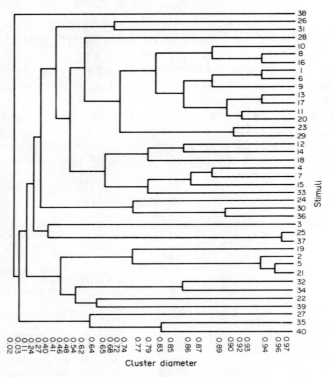

FIG. 5.4   Cluster solution for overlaps among categorical terms.

Just as it is possible to form a matrix of overlap coefficients and summarize the connections among the categorical terms via clustering, so we can also form a matrix of inclusion coefficients and organize them. Table 5.2 shows part of such a matrix, with the inclusion coefficients for categories 01, 06 and 17 ("assisting", "lending a hand" and "aiding"). The complete matrix is in the Appendix. Recall that a value for *Ikj* of greater than 0.5 indicates that category *k* is primarily contained in category *j*, it is evident from Table 5.2 that these three categories are very inclusive of virtually all the others, but that they neither strongly include nor are included by each other. Thus, they belong at the top of the taxonomic hierarchy, and on the same level. A computer routine was written to proceed in this fashion to assign all categories to a rank in the hierarchy of inclusion. Table 5.3 shows the 40 categories in their final hierarchical positions.

TABLE 5.2   *Inclusion coefficients* for categories 01, 06 and 17*

Category	(Assisting) 01	(Lending a hand) 06	(Aiding) 17
01	1.00	0.47	0.50
02	0.78	0.83	0.85
03	0.98	0.95	0.97
04	0.86	0.89	0.91
05	0.71	0.77	0.74
06	0.53	1.00	0.53
07	0.89	0.94	0.91
08	0.75	0.79	0.76
09	0.81	0.77	0.78
10	0.85	0.83	0.84
11	0.72	0.71	0.75
12...	0.75...	0.84...	0.79...
17...	0.50...	0.47...	1.00...

* Inclusion coefficient values range from 0 to 1, with values above 0.5 indicating that the row category includes the column category and values near 0.5 indicating that the row and column categories neither include nor are included by one another.

TABLE 5.3   *Hierarchy* of categories*

Hierarchy level	Categories
1	17, 06, 01
2	13, 16
3	11
4	09, 08, 21
5	10, 12, 05
6	20, 04, 15, 02
7	26, 23, 29, 14, 18, 07, 33, 30
8	28
9	31, 19, 35, 36
10	40, 25
11	03, 24, 32, 34
12	22, 37
13	27, 38, 39

* Hierarchy here refers to how general or inclusive a category is, with categories at the top of the list (level 1) being the most inclusive on down to the bottom (level 13) which contains the least inclusive (most specific) categories.

The main limitation in the hierarchy information is that it alone does not reveal which lower-echelon categories are true subsets of their higher echelon counterparts. Is "rescuing", for instance, a proper subset of "co-operating"? This makes little sense, because according to their overlap coefficient, they are not seen by judges to be synonymous. What is needed is a way to combine the hierarchy and overlap information to give a truly hierarchical taxonomy of semantically related clusters.

Such a combination has been produced in Figure 5.5. Strongly connected clusters are outlined with a solid line, weaker ones with a dashed line. In cases where there are notable links between clusters, or from a member of one cluster to another, these links are indicated by straight lines (solid or dashed, depending on the strength of the overlap). The vertical position of each term in the Figure represents its position in the hierarchy. Thus, for instance, 01, 06 and 17 are arranged at the top; it also turns out that they are highly semantically related (see their clustering positions in Figure 5.4).

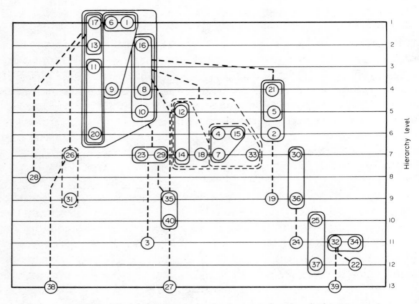

FIG. 5.5 Hierarchical taxonomic clusters of categorical terms.

Before going on to interpret the diagram in Figure 5.5, a couple of structural properties are worth noting. First, it is evident that while proximity in the hierarchy is somewhat associated with semantic overlap, it is by no means strictly so. This fact vindicates the idea of using inclusion as the basis for hierarchy rather than similarity. Secondly, unlike ordinary tree-diagrams, subclusters in this system may have "shirt-tail" subsets which are nevertheless not strong members of the larger cluster to which the subcluster belongs. Thus, for example, the cluster containing categories 2, 5 and 21 is strongly linked to the subcluster containing 16 and 8, but not to the larger cluster to which 16 and 8 belong.

For an interpretation of the taxonomy displayed above, we shall start from the left and top, and work down and to the right. At the top level in the hierarchy, there is a large cluster of terms which contains three smaller subclusters. The subcluster which contains categories 17, 13, 11 and 20 ("aiding", "altruistic", "giving" and "benefiting") is probably best labelled an "altruistic aid" cluster. Its nearest neighbour, which includes 1, 6 and 9 ("assisting", "lending a hand" and "co-operating"), could be named an "assistance" cluster. The "altruistic aid" and "assistance" clusters are strongly connected, at the 0.86 overlap level. The third member of the large cluster contains 16, 8 and 10 ("showing kindness", "being charitable" and "empathizing") and could be labelled "kindness". All terms in the large cluster obviously are central to people's concepts of helping, and have elements of assistance and altruism.

The subcluster containing 16 and 8 (part of the "kindness" cluster) is interesting because it has several "shirt-tail" clusters which are more strongly connected to it than to the other members of the large cluster. Beginning at the left, we have a cluster which includes categories 35 and 40 ("nursing" and "nurturing"). The connection between this cluster and the concept of charitability or kindness seems obvious. The "nurturance" cluster is also connected with the cluster containing 23 and 29 ("ministering to" and "succouring"), which in turn is connected to the entire large cluster.

However, the next pair of clusters is interesting in that it represents a very different aspect of kindness. The first of these includes 12, 14 and 18 ("solving", "taking care of" and "enabling") and thus could be said to represent a "solutions" cluster. The other contains 4, 15, 7 and 33 ("rescuing" "intervening", "saving" and "fixing") and is probably best labelled "heroic intervention". These two contrast vividly in some respects with the "succouring" and "nurturance" clusters, and also with the last cluster which is connected with the "kindness" group. This one includes 21, 5 and 2 ("generous", "sharing" and "donating") and is obviously a "generosity" cluster.

Other "shirt-tails" connected with the large central cluster are category 28 ("collaborating with") and the loosely-knit group containing 26 and 31 ("giving information" and "educating"), which we may term an "educative" cluster. The remaining clusters are those which did not connect strongly with the central cluster. The first of these, containing 30, 36 and 24 ("encouraging", "reinforcing", and "inspiring"), could be called a "reinforcement" cluster. It is possible that this group pertains primarily to the region of unstudied helping behaviours, a conjecture which will be examined later in this chapter. The next group includes 25 and 37 ("comforting" and "consoling") and therefore concerns "emotional support". Finally, we have the group with 32 and 34 at the top ("defending" and "shielding from"), which is apparently a "defence" cluster, especially when one considers that 22 and 39 ("freeing" and "exonerating") are attached to it.

Regional Interpretations of the MDS Model

In the taxonomy in the preceding section, several distinct clusters of categorical terms emerged. These clusters probably represent salient types of helping which figure prominently in subjects' cognitive schema. It makes some sense, then, to map these clusters as contours into the MDS space derived in Chapter 3, and to use the resulting maps to supplement the dimensional interpretations of the MDS model. Given the relatively small sample size on which these data are based, the following analysis must necessarily be exploratory and tentative in nature.

Starting with the most general terms ("assisting", "lending a hand", and "aiding"), it is reasonable to ask whether these categories cover the space uniformly. It might turn out, for instance, that certain kinds of helping forms are sufficiently specialized or peripheral that they are not seen by most people to be very good examples of assistance or aid. Figure 5.6 shows the contour map for the fuzzy-set union of these three categories, in the D1–D3 plane. The interesting feature of this map is the tendency for the exemplars of these general terms to be split into two fairly distinct regions. The two regions correspond to the unstudied and well-studied areas of helping (see Chapter 3), indicating perhaps that there are two types of assistance or aid: the sort which is relatively anonymous and given either to friends or strangers, and another kind which is personal in nature and given primarily to friends. If this split were to hold up with more data from a greater variety of subjects, it could have some far-reaching implications for the study of helping behaviour, since among other things it might point to two distinct sets of social norms concerning assistance or aid.

This finding should also caution researchers about the uncritical use of seemingly broad categories. We began this study by generating a sample of episodes which subjects generally agreed were exemplary of "helping", the master category used in this research programme. But there is no reason to presuppose that the ordinary person's concept of helping is unitary or even coherent. Indeed, much of the analysis thus far suggests that there are some important distinctions people make among behaviours which they nevertheless class together as helping. The fact that even very general terms for helping do not cover the space uniformly indicates that some of these distinctions may be disjunctive, perhaps noting radical discontinuities in social norms, values, or perceptions within the episode space. Chapters 6 and 7 investigate some of these disjunctions, posing the question of whether it is ultimately scientifically meaningful to treat helping as if it represents a unified, distinct area of inquiry.

Similar patterns emerge for the three most general subclusters. The contour map for the "altruistic aid" cluster (the fuzzy-set union of

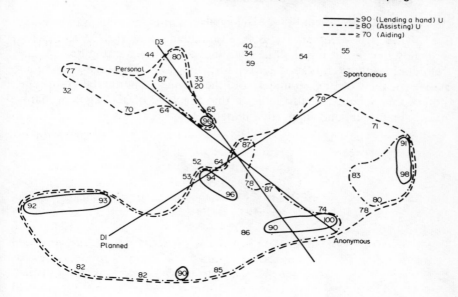

FIG. 5.6   Contour map of the union of "Assisting", "Lending a hand", and 'Aiding" in the D1–D3 planes.

categories 17, 13, 11 and 20) contains the same bifurcated regions, one covering the entire region of well-studied help, and the other concentrated in the serious quadrant of the unstudied region. Likewise, the "assistance" cluster and the "kindness" cluster both exhibit the same two-region split. These patterns are indicative of the distinctiveness of the unstudied region, and suggest that it may involve different social norms from those in the well-studied region. Chapter 6 presents some empirical investigations of this notion.

From Chapter 3 and corroborative evidence from Chapter 4, we know that the unstudied region is distinguished from other types of helping primarily by being personal, given to friends only, and internally motivated. Can the categorical information provide any further insight into the nature of this region? Of course, some of the categories have exemplars unique to the unstudied region, since the existence of unrepresented helping terms was the original motivation for developing a new set of helping forms to be included for analysis with those taken from the social psychological literature. But some of these (such as categories 35 and 40, which make up the "nurturing" cluster) have too few exemplars to fully cover the new region, and others (such as 23 and 29, which comprise the "succouring" category) have too many partial examples in the well-studied region to distinguish that region from the new area.

As it turns out, two clusters do characterize the new region reasonably well. The "reinforcement" cluster (containing categories 30 and 36) is probably the best at this, and its contour map is shown in Figure 5.7. The connotations that terms such as "reinforcing" and "encouraging" have for native speakers of English underscore the original dimensional interpretation of this region, but also indicate that this kind of helping is probably mainly emotional and supportive in nature.

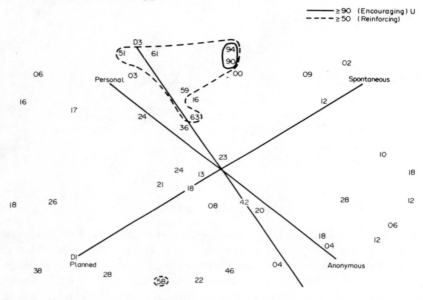

FIG. 5.7 Contour map of the union of "Encouraging" and "Reinforcing" in the D1–D3 plane.

An interesting addendum to this interpretation is provided by the "defence" cluster (the fuzzy-set intersection of categories 32 and 34). Despite the few exemplars for this cluster, it seems plain that they are in that part of the new region which tends toward the serious forms of helping. This probably represents the "doing" component of the new region, and again reinforces the notion that these forms of helping are intimate and personal.

Summary and Implications

In this chapter we have demonstrated methods for constructing refined questionnaire and attitude-scale items, through the use of fuzzy-set concepts. This approach has been predicted on the notion that people's social norms about helping are reflected in the linguistic categories used for denoting different kinds of helping, and that it is therefore important to determine which regions of the MDS space are referenced by a given helping term. This knowledge would be crucial for studies of norms and attributions. In cases where the researcher wishes to construct a question or scale which invokes a specific region of helping in the minds of respondents, the methods presented in this chapter may be used to find the clearest term for such uses.

An exploratory study of people's cognitive taxonomies of helping was also presented, the results of which tended to corroborate and extend the properties of the MDS model developed in Chapters 3 and 4. Again, fuzzy-set concepts were employed to generate a new kind of hierarchy in taxonomic clustering which is well suited to representing linguistic taxonomies.

The importance of the clustering approach lies in the contention that people tend to think in semi-discrete categories rather than in continuous dimensions of the type used in the MDS model, so that the clusters which emerge from a cluster analysis may well represent salient groups of helping terms. The salience of such groups probably in turn reflects special properties of the cluster members, such as the social norms pertaining to them. It was felt that these clusters and their hierarchical relationships with one another would lend additional insights into the cognitive distinctions people make among different forms of helping. Indeed, the resultant taxonomy supported the claim that there is an unstudied region of helping with special features that set it apart in people's minds from other kinds of helping. It also underscored the distinction people seem to draw between giving and doing, although it indicated that both are seen as particular aspects of kindness. Finally, the taxonomy confirmed the intuition that there are several very general terms for helping, and that these are closely related to one another. These general terms do not map well into the MDS space via PREFMAP techniques, since they are bi-regional and therefore not well represented even by the most general distance model in PREFMAP. This bi-regionality points to a possibly dual nature of helping, which will be further investigated in Chapter 7.

The clusters and hierarchy suggested by the taxonomy should provide some theoretical tools for a meaningful classification of helping and eventually for sophisticated theoretical statements. In fact, they are likely to lead to a conditional view of helping behaviour. For example, the search for the "helping personality" might be rejuvenated by entertaining the hypothesis that different personality types are well suited to different kinds of helping, or that personality factors make more of a difference for some kinds of helping than for others. These and other related possibilities will be explored in Chapters 6 and 7.

6

Implications of the Helping Taxonomy for Studying Behaviour

P. R. AMATO

THIS CHAPTER discusses applications of the helping taxonomy to the study of prosocial behaviour. Cognitions are, of course, both interesting and important enough to be studied in their own right. Nevertheless, most social psychologists are probably interested, ultimately, in what people do, not just in what they think or say. This chapter will present three different strategies for applying the helping taxonomy to the study of behaviour.

The first, and most traditional strategy, is to take an experimental approach. An investigator using this approach can construct situations which vary along one or more dimensions of the taxonomy. For example, situations requiring intimate forms of help can be compared with situations requiring more anonymous forms of assistance. By holding constant other aspects of the situation, the effect of this dimension (or any other) on some aspect of behaviour could be determined. The second strategy involves the use of the taxonomy to classify everyday helping behaviours in natural settings. In this manner, the naturally occurring distribution of various types of helping could be compared across a number of social contexts. The third strategy involves exploring the expectations of behaviour which people have for helping episodes in various regions of the helping space. If people do cognitively differentiate helping episodes into various types, one would expect the normative structure of these types to vary accordingly.

In this chapter the results from three separate studies will be presented, one representing each of the general strategies outlined above. Before presenting this material, however, a few general issues in relating cognitions to behaviour will be discussed.

Relating Cognition to Helping Behaviour

The research presented in Chapters 2, 3 and 4 indicated that people possess stable cognitive structures of helping which can be reliably represented as meaningful regions in a four-dimensional space. Furthermore, there appeared to be a substantial degree of consistency between different social groups in the cognitive schema they used to differentiate among instances of helping. However, while it is one thing to identify and describe the schema people carry around in their heads, it is fair to ask whether these implicit structures are actually related to behaviour. It is quite possible that these perceptions of helping types are convenient stereotypes which people draw upon when asked to make a distinction, yet their power to affect actual behaviour may be over-ridden by more salient but unanticipated characteristics of situations.

This is an important question, and it is likely that a large number of social psychologists would be quite sceptical about the importance of a cognitive model such as the one developed in this volume in understanding overt behaviour. There appears to be a general mistrust of the layperson's view among social psychologists, and a reluctance to explain behaviour by reference to what people say about their behaviour. According to this position, people are often only vaguely aware of the psychodynamic or situational forces which affect their behaviour. Furthermore, people may have little or no access to their higher thought processes (Nisbett and Wilson, 1977). Therefore, if people are asked why they act in a certain manner, they are likely to respond with simplistic sterotypes and misconceptions based upon *a priori* causal theories. The psychologist, on the other hand, is able to take into account in a more "objective" fashion the complex interplay of variables which determine behaviour (see Harré and Secord, 1972, Chap. 6, for a discussion and an alternative point of view).

While this is a widely held view in social psychology, the classic work of Latané and Darley (1970) did a lot to foster this notion specifically in the field of helping-behaviour research. Their seminal work on bystander intervention appears to contain two different implicit sets of assumptions about the relationship between cognition and behaviour. At times, cognition is seen as being of some importance in explaining behaviour. In fact, Latané and Darley's well-known decision-making model of bystander intervention gives a prominent place to a cognitive variable: the individual's definition of the situation. Latané and Darley argued that before a person will intervene, he or she must define the situation as an emergency and assume personal responsibility for acting. However, in this model, the bystander's definition of the situation is not a function of his understanding of the helping process, awareness of social norms of appropriate behaviour, values or personality. Instead, the bystander's cognitions are the product of powerful situational cues which lead the person to perceive the situation in a certain way. Thus, the presence of non-responsive others can lead the individual to define the situation as a non-emergency, a situation not requiring intervention. From this perspective, perception is passive and cognitions are simply intervening variables between behaviour and its ultimate cause, situations (Latané and Darley, 1970, p. 81).

Other aspects of the work of Latané and Darley, however, suggest a second model of cognition and behaviour, a model which strongly discredits the validity of cognitively based explanations of helping. Latané and Darley claimed that people are generally very poor predictors of their own behaviour in certain helping situations. As part of their research they questioned people about their likely behaviour in a hypothetical situation involving an epileptic suffering a severe seizure and found that virtually everyone replied that they would definitely offer assistance. However, when experimental subjects were placed in a laboratory situation where they were able to diffuse responsibility onto other (imagined) bystanders, the majority of subjects did not help. Furthermore, after the episode was concluded, subjects did not appear to have a clear understanding of why they had behaved as they did. Most subjects seriously underestimated the extent to which their behaviour had been inhibited by the (imagined) presence of others.

Other research (Latané and Darley, 1970) which involved subjects filling out a questionnaire while children in the next room simulated a serious fight suggested that most subjects failed to intervene, then rationalized their lack of intervention by defining the situation as non-serious. When subjects were given a good excuse not to intervene, they generally defined the situation as quite serious. This second implicit model in Latané and Darley's work suggests that situations determine behaviour directly (perhaps in conjunction with unconscious motivations) and cognitions such as the definition of the situation are simply after-the-fact rationalizations or epiphenomena.

Taken together with the fact that Latané and Darley obtained no significant correlations between a number of seemingly relevant personality variables and helping, this body or research appeared to lead to a firm conclusion: behaviour is under the control of powerful characteristics of situations. It followed that the identification of these situational determinants of helping was the most important task facing social psychologists working in this area. Explanations for behaviour located solely within the individual were to be avoided. This set of assumptions dominated much helping-behaviour research for nearly a decade. Although cognitive variables were still studied by researchers (see Chapter 1), cognitions were generally seen, at best, as being mediating variable between situations and behaviour (Lau and Blake, 1976) and, at worst, as being downright misleading.

Ultimately, this proliferation of situational studies began to generate problems. First, the plethora of situational variables which research had linked to helping became increasingly difficult to integrate conceptually. The number of situational characteristics which could influence certain types of helping in certain contexts and the interactions between them appeared to be infinite (Morgan, 1973). Clearly, some model was needed to guide the search for relevant variables.

A second problem concerns the increasing realization among many social psychologists that research dealing with situations has been too one-sided. Ultimately, social behaviour is too complex to be determined by one set of variables only, and the detailed study of situations, at the expense of individual differences, has proved ultimately to be inadequate and unsatisfying (see Krebs, 1978, for a discussion). A number of psychologists have argued for a more comprehensive point of view in which characteristics of individuals and characteristics of situations are studied together so that the interaction between the two can be determined (Bem and Allen, 1974; Bowers, 1973; Endler and Magnusson, 1976; Rushton, 1980; Staub, 1978; Forgas, 1980). This trend is consistent with the current development in social psychology of a more cognitive model of human behaviour and an increasing concern with social episodes (Forgas, 1980).

An increased emphasis on cognition allows a reanalysis of much of Latané and Darley's work. Backman (1979) argued that Latané and Darley did not pay sufficient attention to the problem of consensual validation of the meaning of the situation by the research participants. Since the subjects in the epileptic-seizure experiment were not in communication with anyone else, they were in a highly ambiguous situation concerning what was happening in the laboratory. It could be argued that many subjects were waiting for clearer cues from other experimental participants before assisting. Since such cues (e.g. the slamming of doors, further cries for help, requests for direct assistance from other subjects, a call for help by the experimenter) were non-existent, it is not surprising that subjects had great difficulty in arriving at a clear definition of the situation. Alternative definitions may have been in terms of an elaborate joke by another student or the experimenter, an attention-gaining act by a somewhat disturbed student, or an experimental simulation.

As Moscovici (1976) has argued in relation to conformity studies, actors in ambiguous and uncertain situations are forced to take into account the judgements of others, that is, to organize and evaluate the shared intersubjectivities of the group before responding. It is not difficult to appreciate that subjects in Latané and Darley's study, prevented as they were from communicating with fellow subjects, were thus in the invidious position of having to take into account others' views of the episode but not being able to obtain these views. It can be proposed therefore that the delays in helping and the lower rates of helping reported were not simply due to the variable of group size on ascription of responsibility, but to the effect of this manipulation on the cognitive understandings of the research participants. It is argued here that a more cognitive view of the behaviour of these subjects is not inconsistent with the interpretations which Latané and Darley themselves made. However, while this cognitive approach is implicit in their work, it has not been developed and elaborated upon as much as the "situational" side of their paradigm.

A final problem which results from an overconcern with situations relates to the fact that the situational model of human behaviour is intimately tied to the dominant research method of traditional social psychology: the laboratory experiment. The usual procedure in laboratory experimentation is for a researcher to randomly allocate subjects to either an experimental or a control group, vary some characteristic of the situation and then record the (helping) behaviour of subjects. Significant differences between conditions implies that situational differences have accounted for variance in behaviour. However, when attempting to generalize to social behaviour outside the laboratory, serious problems emerge. In everyday life, individuals are not allocated to situations by experimenters; people actively choose the situations they wish to become involved in. Volunteering to become a telephone counsellor at a community centre, dropping by the hospital to donate blood, or visiting a friend because he might be lonely are all helping situations that an individual intentionally chooses to enter. Once in the situation, it is quite possible that the circumstances at hand will strongly influence behaviour, even in ways which are unanticipated or only partially understood. But the decision to enter, or leave, the situation is still up to the actor. This being so, people's expectations about a situation, their understanding of the relevant social norms and "rules", their anticipation of the demands which will be made on them and the benefits which might accrue to them will all strongly influence the individual's decision to get involved or initiate certain types of helping activities. This general line of thought is supported in research by Furnham (1981) who found that personality variables strongly predicted preferences for certain types of situations. Furnham argued that in everyday life situations are largely a function of the personal characteristics of individuals. Indeed, as Bowers (1973) has stated, "Situations are as much a product of the person as the person's behaviour is a function of the situation" (p. 327).

These sorts of considerations are probably much less important in the typical laboratory experiment in which the individual finds himself in an unusual and artificial situation, a situation not of his making and over which he has little control. It is not surprising that under such highly constrained circumstances, situational cues are so powerful. The work of Latané and Darley (1970) with emergency situations is, in this sense, quite valid, for emergencies are highly unusual events over which people have little control. Thus, situational cues, like the behaviour of other bystanders, are likely to be highly salient. It is argued here, however, that this is not the best model for understanding most everyday helping.

Nevertheless, a cognitively based taxonomy could still be of considerable use to social psychologists committed to an experimental methodology. Ultimately, findings from experimental research could be used to supplement knowledge gained from naturalistic and cognitive studies of helping. It is unlikely, though, that experimental research, by itself, will be sufficient for an understanding of everyday helping.

Using the Taxonomy in Experimental Work

There are two ways in which the helping taxonomy can be used by experimental social psychologists. The first use is based upon the assumption that since the dimensions of the taxonomy are psychologically salient for individuals, then helping situations varied systematically along one or more of the cognitive dimensions should produce corresponding variation in behaviour as well. Experiments investigating this possibility could devise helping situations which varied, say, in the degree of intimacy involved, and then record the behaviour of subjects in each of these conditions. Following this sort of procedure, the experimenter would be using the dimensions of the taxonomy as independent variables. An important step in this procedure would be for the experimenter to later determine whether subjects perceived the situation as having the characteristics which the experimenter intended (for example, intimacy or anonymity), since it would be the subject's definition of the situation, not the experimenter's, which would determine the subject's behaviour.

A few studies have, in fact, done something like this. Research conducted by Staub and Baer (1974), Ashton and Severy (1976) and Shotland and Huston (1979) looked at the likelihood of people helping in situations differing in seriousness. The general finding of these studies is that people are more likely to help in more serious situations. Thus, this one dimension of cognitive salience, seriousness, has already been shown to have important behavioural implications. There is no reason why researchers could not do similar experiments comparing spontaneous with planned help, intimate with anonymous help, and giving with doing help. Going a step further, two or more dimensions could be combined into a factorial design to look for possible interactions between conditions.

A second general strategy might be more useful for researchers who are not interested in studying the behavioural effects of the cognitive dimensions as such, but who wish to make intelligent choices about what forms of helping behaviour to incorporate into their own research. Frequently, researchers include a number of helping measures in a single experiment in an attempt to get a more general picture of the effect of some independent variable on helping. However, without a taxonomy to guide the choice of helping forms, the researcher has to rely on intuitive judgement to ensure that he or she has sampled from different categories of behaviour.

Consider a hypothetical researcher who uses three different forms of helping as dependent variables: returning a lost letter, helping a confederate pick up dropped packages, and giving directions to someone on the street. While the researcher might feel that he has sampled a variety of helping forms, the taxonomic model presented in this volume indicates that, as far as people's perceptions are concerned, these three helping forms are basically the same type of helping, that is, they are all spontaneous, non-serious, anonymous, doing forms of helping. If the researcher finds that all three forms of helping yield similar results, he or she will probably conclude that the relationship between the independent variable and helping is a fairly general one. Consideration of the taxonomic model suggests that the researcher has not established the generality of the findings at all.

A taxonomy can be used to help guarantee that a researcher is sampling from a representative range of helping forms. If the researcher then finds differences between one measure of helping and the next, he or she will be in a better position to interpret, or at least suggest plausible hypotheses about why these differences occurred. This is because the researcher knows ahead of time how the various forms of helping are related to each other in a larger framework.

An extended example will now be presented illustrating this application. The second author was interested in looking at urban–rural differences in helping behaviour. A number of studies had previously been done in this area, but the results are inconsistent. The usual procedure in most of this research is for some situation to be set up in both large cities and small towns in which people have the chance to either help or not. Rates of helping in the two kinds of areas are then statistically compared. A literature review revealed that out of a total of 18 studies dealing with this question, nine found that urbanites were less helpful than ruralites (Amato, 1981; House and Wolf, 1978; Korte and Ayvalioglu, 1981; Levine *et al*, 1976; Korte and Kerr, 1975; Gelfand *et al*, 1973; Merrens, 1973; Rushton, 1978; Takooshian, Haber and Lucido, 1977). Out of the remaining nine studies, five found that urbanites were more helpful than ruralites (Amato, 1978; Hansson and Slade, 1977; Hansson and Slade, 1978; Forbes and Gromoll, 1971; Weiner, 1976), and four found no difference (Korte, Ypma and Toppen 1975; Krupat and Coury, 1975; Rotton, 1977; Schneider and Mockus, 1975).

These inconsistencies in the literature are probably due to a number of problems. First, there is a problem with the sampling of areas. In most of the studies cited above, no attempt was made to get a random, or even representative, sample of urban and rural areas. Furthermore, different researchers have sampled geographical areas along different ranges of the urban–rural continuum, thus making comparisons between studies exceedingly difficult.

A second major problem refers not to the sampling of areas, but to the sampling of helping behaviours. Since these studies used different measures of helping, it is not surprising that different relationships between urbanism and helping rates were found. Also, there is no assurance that all of these studies, taken in combination, have sampled across the entire range of helping forms. To overcome some of these problems, a large-scale study was planned to compare rates of helping in urban and rural areas of Australia. This study included both a random sample of geographical areas and a systematic sample of helping behaviours derived from the helping taxonomy.

Method

A stratified random sample of cities and towns in two states was taken, the sample being stratified on the basis of population size and degree of isolation (distance from a large, capital city). The final sample consisted of 61 cities and towns which covered a geographical range of approximately one-third of the country.

The three-dimensional model of helping described in Chapter 2 was used to choose a sample of helping measures, the intention being to choose one helping form from each region of the space. Six helping behaviours were therefore needed, one from the extreme end of each of the three dimensions (at the time this study was planned, the personal–anonymous dimension had not yet been discovered). Four helping behaviours were initially chosen. "Correcting inaccurate directions which you have over-heard being given to a stranger" was chosen from the spontaneous extreme of the planned–spontaneous dimension. In this situation, the investigator walked into a store and asked directions from a shopper (confederate). The confederate gave obviously incorrect directions, and the behaviour of the shop assistant, standing within hearing range, was recorded (i.e. did or did not correct the inaccurate information). "Writing your favourite colour for a student working on a class project" was chosen from the non-serious end of the seriousness dimension. In this situation the investigator approached pedestrians on the sidewalk, explained that he was a university student, and asked them to write their favourite colour on a sheet of paper. Whether the subject complied with the request or not was recorded. For an active, doing form of helping, "picking up fallen cards" was chosen. In this situation, the investigator dropped a handful of envelopes in front of a pedestrian chosen to be the subject. Whether the subject helped to pick up the envelopes or not was recorded. For the passive, giving form of helping, "giving a donation to the Multiple Sclerosis Society" was chosen. In this situation, researchers working as official collectors for the Multiple Sclerosis Society, and wearing identifying badges, approached pedestrians in the downtown area with the intention of selling one dollar packets of greeting cards. Whether the subject purchased a packet of cards or not was recorded.

A problem arose, however, because none of the situations at the seriousness pole of dimension 2 or the planned, formal pole of dimension 1 seemed appropriate for field-work purposes. Therefore, two new helping behaviours had to be invented. The serious situation consisted of a pedestrian walking along the street with a noticeable limp. Suddenly he would fall to the ground with a cry of pain, and while lying there, would reveal a heavily bandaged leg smeared with fresh theatrical blood. The actor would continue to lie on the ground until the pedestrian chosen to be the subject either offered assistance or completely passed by. For the measure of planned, formal helping, an already existing data set was utilized: non-response rates to the 1976 Australian census. For this purpose, non-response rates were conceptualized as behaviour indicating a lack of co-operation with the federal government, while properly completed forms were conceptualized as co-operative, helpful behaviour. Before using these two measures, however, ratings were obtained on the appropriate dimensional characteristics from a sample of six raters. In this way the situations could be "mapped" back into the multidimensional helping space. The two new situations emerged in the areas we had anticipated: the bloody-leg situation appeared close to the end of the seriousness pole of dimension 2 while completing the census forms accurately and fully was seen as a planned, formal type of helping at the extreme end of dimension 1 (see Figure 6.1). This step in the research process indicates, interestingly, that the taxonomy can be used not only to choose previously studied forms of helping, but to generate new helping forms which have certain desired characteristics.

Response–non-response rates for the census questionnaires were obtained for the 61 cities and towns in the sample from the Australian Bureau of Statistics. For the other five situations, data were gathered by a research team which visited each of the areas (six of the towns had to be omitted due to extraneous circumstances such as weather, accidents, etc.). Each of the five situations was enacted approximately five times in each location. The number of times each episode was enacted were: correcting inaccurate directions $n = 292$), hurt-leg situation ($n = 226$), multiple-sclerosis purchase ($n = 276$), colour request ($n = 292$), dropped envelopes ($n = 271$). Full details of the methods used can be found in Amato (1982).

Results

For data analytic purposes, the cities and towns were ordered into five levels of population size: less than 1000 people, 1000 to 4999 people, 5000 to 19,999 people, 20,000 to 300,000 people, and 1,000,000 people or more

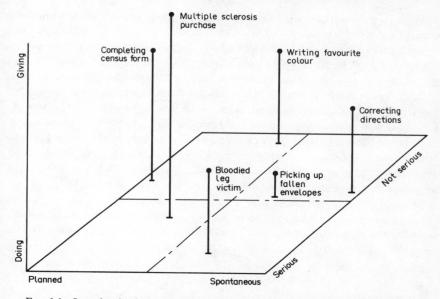

FIG. 6.1   Location in three-dimensional episode space of the six helping episodes selected for research.

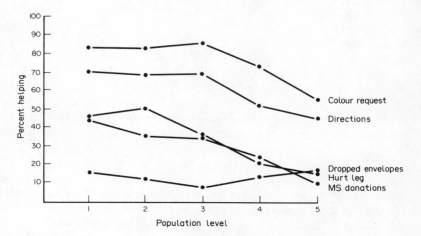

FIG. 6.2   Percent of people helping at five levels of population size, for five measures of helping.

(there were no cities in the sample between the fourth and fifth level). The percentage of people helping for each of the five behavioural measures at each level of population size is displayed in Figure 6.2.

With four of the five measures of helping (correcting inaccurate directions, writing your favourite colour, donating to the Multiple Sclerosis Fund, and helping the hurt-leg victim) there were significant negative associations between city size and helping. For the fifth measure (picking up dropped envelopes) there was no significant relationship with city size.

A different result was obtained from the census questionnaire measure. Figure 6.3 reveals that response rates were lowest in the smallest towns, i.e. those towns having less than 1000 people. The amount of co-operative behaviour then increases with city size until one gets to the largest cities, where the response rate drops somewhat. (The census response score reported here is a factor score based upon the percent of people in each area answering eight main questions on the census form.) The same relationship, with small towns having the lowest rates of response, remained even after a large number of other variables were partialled out, including various educational and social-class indices, and distance from a large city (isolation).

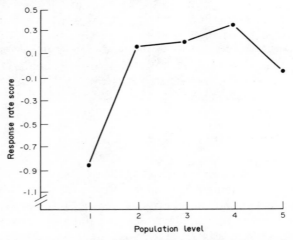

FIG. 6.3   Response rate scores for the 1976 Australian census at five levels of population size.

The correlations between helping and population level and distance from a capital city (isolation) are given in Table 6.1. It can be noted that the correlations between helping and city size are negative and significant for the first four helping forms. Likewise, the correlations between distance from a capital city and helping are generally positive. Helping in the dropped-envelopes situation, however, correlates close to zero with both urban–rural variables, while the census-response score correlates positively with size and negatively with isolation (the correlation with isolation is only marginally significant, $p = 0.08$).

TABLE 6.1   *Pearsonian product-moment correlations between six measures of helping and city population and distance from a capital city (isolation)*

Helping form	Population	Isolation	n
Correcting inaccurate directions	−0.21***	0.12*	288
Hurt-leg victim	−0.28***	0.19**	226
M. S. donation	−0.25***	0.21***	276
Colour request	−0.26***	0.10	292
Dropped envelopes	0.04	−0.00	271
Census-responses rate	0.34**	−0.22	61 (cities)

* p <0.05 (two-tailed)	** p <0.01 (two-tailed)	*** p <0.001 (two-tailed)

What can be concluded from this data? First, in four out of six situations, people in small towns were, indeed, more helpful than people in big cities. To this extent, the popular stereotype of the unhelpful urbanite is supported. However, one can also make statements about the limitations of this effect. It did not occur in all situations, and with one measure of helpfulness, people in small towns helped less than urbanites. The position of this "deviant" situation in the helping model might give clues about the proper interpretation of this finding. It is possible that ruralites are generally more helpful when it comes to situations requiring informal casual, spontaneous behaviour. However, a form of helping such as filling out a census form, which is impersonal, formalized, planned, and even bureaucratized, might be an alien kind of helping which people in rural communities are not familar with. As such, ruralites might resent the demands placed upon their time, be doubtful about the value of the exercise, and even be suspicious about its purpose. This hypothesis could be tested with a further study.

Another point worth noting concerns the personal–anonymous dimension. Because this dimension was not included in the study, all the forms of helping reported here fall into the anonymous region of the helping space. However, a number of studies have been conducted investigating behaviour between friends in urban and rural settings. The general finding from this research appears to be that urbanites have just as many friends, see them as often, and are as close to them as are ruralites (Reiss, 1959; Key, 1968; Sutcliffe and Crabbe, 1963; Kasarda and Janowitz, 1974; Franck, 1980). This suggests that rates of personal helping, the kind of help one is more likely to give to a friend, may be the same in rural and urban areas. If this is true, it means that the unhelpfulness of urbanites is limited to those forms of helping in the anonymous region of the taxonomy.

In summary, the use of the taxonomic model offers the following advantages to experimentally minded researchers: (1) The model gives the researcher a framework from which to sample behaviours. It thus helps ensure that the researcher does not choose helping measures which overlap, and allows him or her to sample across a wider range of different forms of behaviour. (2) The taxonomy can be useful in generating new helping forms for study such that the researcher knows ahead of time the important characteristics these forms possess and how they are related to other forms of helping. (3) The taxonomy provides a framework within which the researcher can begin to explain differences and similarities between the results of different experiments. Apparent inconsistencies between results might be resolved by specifying the range of conditions to which a finding applies.

Classifying Naturally Occurring Helping Behaviours

Another major application of the helping taxonomy involves the classification of freely occurring forms of behaviour in naturalistic settings. In a sense, the researcher using this technique is acting like a botanist or zoologist who goes out into the field and, with the aid of a taxonomy, records the frequency of various life forms in different habitats. The social psychologist using this strategy would be interested in answering questions such as: What is the distribution of types of naturally occurring helping behaviour in everyday life? What types of helping are very common and what types of helping are very rare? How does the frequency of different types of helping vary in different social contexts? For example, what types of helping are most common in the helping professions, and how might the types of helping most frequently engaged in by, say, social workers differ from the types of helping typically engaged in by clinical psychologists, nurses, or psychiatrists? Similarly, are different types of help typically offered by friends, family and neighbours?

As a first step in this direction, 97 university students enrolled in behavioural science courses at James Cook University of North Queensland produced lists of the occasions they could think of during the last week in which they had helped someone. After about 10 minutes, most students were able to generate four and six episodes, resulting in a sample of 475 incidents of helping. Examples of these helping episodes include "Helping a friend move house", "Giving an acquaintance a lift to the university", and "loaned my lecture notes to a person in one of my classes". The taxonomic scheme was then explained to these people, and they were asked to return to each helping behaviour they had listed and categorize it as being either planned or spontaneous, serious or non-serious, personal or anonymous, and doing or giving. For the sake of simplicity, each of the dimensions was treated as a dichotomy (in fact, there is reason to believe that when people think about helping they have actually been involved in, they think to some extent in terms of discrete dichotomies. This evidence is discussed in Chapter 5.)

Verbal descriptions were given to make the meanings of the terms less ambiguous. Planned help was described as help which had been thought about ahead of time as opposed to spontaneous help which was more casual, unstructured and occurred with little or no prior warning. Serious help was described as help in which the situation had important, possibly grave consequences for the person in need while non-serious help was described as help in which the person's need was less important, less critical, and perhaps quite trivial. Personal help was described as intimate, close and personally involving as opposed to anonymous help which was less intimate, less close and could have been given just as easily to a stranger as to a friend. Doing help was described as active intervention-type helping in which you make something happen for someone, while giving help was described as a more passive, sharing type of help, especially in which material possessions were involved. Almost without exception, all respondents were able to classify all the helping episodes with extremely little difficulty, suggesting that people found these dichotomous classifications both meaningful and appropriate for the data.

As essential aspect of this procedure was the self-classification of helping behaviour by the people themselves. Since we are working with an emic taxonomy, it would make little sense for the researchers at this stage to impose their own subjective definitions upon people's behaviours. Nevertheless, we did examine the labels people applied to most of the reported episodes. In only a few cases did the classifications seem problematic, for example, in labelling a behaviour such as telling the time to someone as serious. Of course, it is quite possible that within the context of the situation the person's need was important enough to be considered serious. Thus, we did not try to second guess the respondent's own interpretations of the situation or their behaviour.

The frequency of occurrence for each type of help was then tabulated. Overall, 32 percent of the helping episodes were described as planned with 68 percent being described as spontaneous. Non-serious helping was more frequent at 67 versus 33 percent. Episodes involving doing forms of helping were more frequent at 60 percent than were episodes involving giving forms of help at 40 percent. Finally, 70 percent of the helping episodes were described as personal while only 30 percent were described as anonymous.

Perhaps the most surprising finding to emerge at this stage is the high frequency of personal forms of helping. The research reported in Chapter 3 indicated that personal forms of helping have been seriously under-represented in the helping literature. Yet, personal forms of helping make up more than two-thirds of the everyday helping behaviours reported by the respondents. This suggests that most of the research findings reported in the social psychological literature refer to forms of prosocial behaviour which are not typical of most everyday interaction.

The personal forms of helping included incidents such as "Buying lunch for a friend", "Cooking dinner for a flatmate when she was tired and I was going out to eat", "Talking with a depressed friend about his problem", and "Talking with a shy person at a party to try and make the person feel comfortable". Many, but not all, of the personal episodes involved friends or acquaintances. Understandably, these would be difficult forms of behaviour to study experimentally.

It is likely that personal forms of helping were so frequent because most social interaction occurs with friends and family rather with strangers. Inspection of the helping episodes reveals that for many people, even seemingly uninvolving forms of behaviour such as giving someone change for a parking meter, can be rather personal if the recipient is a good friend. The same behaviour exhibited toward a stranger, of course, would be quite impersonal. Thus, personal helping is probably more common simply because most of the time people give help to people that they know well. A similar explanation might be appropriate for the greater frequency of non-serious as opposed to serious forms of help-giving. Although serious situations like "Helped a relative cope with the death of her child" and "Helped an old man who had fallen over on the sidewalk" occurred occasionally in the sample, most helping episodes which occur in everyday life are more mundane and less critical. Thus, the smaller frequency of serious forms of helping probably reflects the fact that serious situations occur less frequently for most people.

Further trends in the data were revealed by breaking down the frequencies into a $2 \times 2 \times 2 \times 2$ contingency table. These data appear in Table 6.2. Note that not only is personal help very common, but planned–personal forms of help are also quite common. While planned–personal forms of helping, as indicated in Chapter 3, are quite rare in the literature on prosocial behaviour, these forms of helping make up a full 27 percent of the sample of everyday behaviours.

The most noticeable trend in Table 6.2 is for anonymous forms of help-giving to be very uncommon, except when the situation is both spontaneous and non-serious, in which case they are quite common (22 per cent). Another way of looking at the data is to say that planned help is more likely to involve a personal, intimate component than is spontaneous help. On the other hand, planned–anonymous forms of help are extremely rare, representing only 5 percent of the total number of behaviours. Thus, there appears to be a natural association between the planned–spontaneous and the personal–anonymous categories. Overall, 85 percent of planned help is also personal, while only 65 percent of spontaneous help is personal. (This is also echoed in the bipolar ratings for all groups, as reported in Chapter 4, in that these two dimensions were moderately correlated.)

TABLE 6.2 *Frequencies of different categories of helping in everyday life as reported and categorized by ninety-seven university students (n = 474 helping episodes)*

		Planned		Spontaneous	
		Serious	Not serious	Serious	Not serious
Personal	Doing	30 (6.3)	53 (11.2)	47 (9.9)	63 (13.3)
	Giving	19 (4.0)	25 (5.3)	35 (7.4)	62 (13.1)
Anonymous	Doing	7 (1.5)	10 (2.1)	8 (1.7)	65 (13.7)
	Giving	4 (0.8)	2 (0.4)	5 (1.1)	39 (8.2)

Numbers in parenthesis refer to percentages of the total number of cases

Another natural association appears to exist between the serious–non-serious and the personal–anonymous categories. While only 64 percent of non-serious help is also personal, 85 percent of serious help is personal. This may reflect the fact that people with serious problems are more likely to go to friends and family for help than they are to go to strangers.

Possible explanations for the other trends in the data will be discussed in the next section where people's normative expectations about various types of helping are explored. It is sufficient to say at this point that preliminary data have revealed certain patterns in everyday helping behaviour. These data can serve as a baseline to compare with frequencies of behaviours derived from other more specialized contexts. To this purpose, self-reports were collected of helping behaviours from a sample of nurses working at a state hospital and a sample of social-work students on field placement. These data will be reported, however, in Chapter 7 where some further implications of the helping taxonomy are discussed.

Exploring People's Expectations of Behaviour: Normative Aspects of Helping Types

The third strategy to be presented involves an investigation of the expectations of behaviour which people hold for forms of helping located in different regions of the helping space. If the dimensions of the helping taxonomy have psychological salience for individuals, then it would be expected that the normative structure of helping forms varied along these dimensions will vary. Indeed, one might ask why people would cognitively differentiate one form of helping from another unless there are important behavioural, affective and motivational differences involved in performing the two types of helping.

As a first step in exploring these normative differences, a questionnaire study was carried out in which subjects were presented with short written descriptions of helping episodes constructed to fall into specific regions of the helping space. Subjects then rated their expectations about these episodes on a number of bipolar scales. In-depth interviews were later conducted with selected respondents to aid in the interpretation of the questionnaire data.

Method

The helping episodes were designed along the lines of a $2 \times 2 \times 2 \times 2$ factorial design with planned versus spontaneous, serious versus non-serious, personal versus anonymous, and doing versus giving as factors. For each of the sixteen cells in the design, helping episodes were constructed which had the desired qualities. As an example, the episode below was designed to represent the spontaneous, non-serious, anonymous, doing condition:

> You are walking along the street and spot a lost letter. It is addressed and has a stamp on it. It is about one block to the nearest post office and you wonder if you should drop it off there.

The episode below was written to represent the planned, serious, personal, giving condition:

> A friends of yours is very depressed these days. You will be going into town to do some shopping later in the day and you consider the possibility of buying your friend a small gift to help cheer him/her up.

It proved to be extremely difficult to compose helping episodes in which only the levels of the four factors were varied while all other aspects of the situations were held constant. While this proved easy to do with only two, and even three factors, adding the fourth factor stretched the writer's imagination to the point where the situations began to appear rather artificial and unrealistic. Thus, the attempt to hold all other situational characteristics strictly constant was abandoned. Instead, not one, but three realistic, good examples of helping episodes representing each of the 16 cells were composed. Subjects then rated each of the three representative episodes from a given cell in the design, and the mean rating for the three was computed. In this way, some of the idiosyncratic differences between the helping situations were averaged out. Care was taken to ensure that no obvious differences (like solicited versus unsolicted help) were confounded with any of the independent variables across the range of episodes.

The subjects in this study were 103 students enrolled in Behavioural

Science courses at James Cook University of North Queensland. Volunteers were randomly allocated to one of the 16 cells in the design and were given the appropriate set of three helping episodes to read. Subjects read the situations and filled out their questionnaires in groups of between 10 and 20 people.

Subjects were asked three questions about each of the three helping episodes. Each question was answered on a 7-point scale. The three questions, and the end points of the scales, are listed below:

1. How obligated would you personally feel to offer this type of help in this situation? (1 = not obligated at all, 7 = very obligated).
2. How many people do you think would help in this situation? (1 = almost no one, 7 = almost everyone).
3. How likely would you be to give this type of help in this situation? (1 = not likely at all, 7 = very likely).

Subjects were also asked to give a global rating of cost involved in helping on a 7-point scale. Finally, a set of manipulation check items was included.

Question 1 was designed to tap the existence of a personal norm for the type of help in question. Question 2 was designed to measure the person's perception of a social norm, that is, the person's expectation of whether most people would, or would not, offer the type of help. The third question asked people to make a prediction about their own behaviour in the situation. While people's self-predictions of helping behaviour have been found to be unreliable (Latané and Darley, 1970), other research suggests that self-predictions may be reliable when looking at everyday, intentional helping behaviour. For example, Pomazal and Jaccard (1976) found a correlation of 0.59 between stated intentions to donate blood in an upcoming blood drive and actual later attempts to donate blood.

In-depth interviews lasting approximately 20 minutes were later carried out with a small sample of six respondents. The purpose of the interview was to more fully probe the reasons underlying people's responses to the questionnaire items. Responses from the interviews were used to help interpret the questionnaire results.

Results and Discussion

A manipulation check was performed to see if subjects perceived the helping episodes as intended. Subjects rated their three episodes on six 7-point scales: spontaneous versus planned help, informal versus formal help, non-serious versus serious help, anonymous versus personal help, the kind of help given to either friends or strangers versus the type of help normally given only to friends, and giving what I have versus doing what I can. The results indicated that the helping episodes were strongly perceived as having the desired characteristics. Overall, the "planned" helping forms were rated higher on the spontaneous–planned scale ($t = 8.57$, df $= 101$, $p < 0.001$) and higher on the informal–formal scale ($t = 3.62$, df $= 99$, $p < 0.001$) than were the "spontaneous" forms. "Serious" helping episodes were rated higher on the non-serious–serious scale ($t = 7.54$, df $= 100$, $p < 0.001$) than were the "non-serious" episodes. "Personal" forms of helping were rated as being higher on both the anonymous–personal scale ($t = 11.95$, df $= 99$, $p < 0.001$) and the friends or strangers versus friends only scale ($t = 8.28$, df $= 100$, $p < 0.001$) than were the "anonymous" forms. Finally, "doing" forms of helping were rated higher on the giving–doing scale ($t = 4.27$, df $= 99$, $p < 0.001$) than were the "giving" forms.

Each of the three questions was treated as a dependent variable in a $2 \times 2 \times 2 \times 2$ factorial analysis of variance. If the distinctions between helping forms suggested by the helping taxonomy are reflected in different normative expectations, then the four factors and their interactions should account for substantial amounts of the variance in people's ratings. This, indeed, appears to be the case. The proportion of variance accounted for by the planned–spontaneous, non-serious–serious, personal–anonymous, and giving–doing factors is 0.39, 0.23 and 0.19 for questions 1, 2 and 3, respectively.

The analysis of variance on the first question dealing with the perception of a moral, personal obligation to help yielded three main effects. First, people reported a stronger obligation to help when the situation was serious than when it was not serious (means $= 4.29$ and 2.85, respectively; $F = 30.79$, df $= 1, 87$, $p < 0.001$). Second, subjects reported a stronger moral obligation to help when the type of help required doing rather than giving (means $= 3.97$ and 3.15, respectively $F = 8.07$, df $= 1, 87$, $p < 0.01$). Third, subjects reported a stronger moral obligation to help when the help was anonymous than when the help was personal (means $= 3.985$ and 3.21, respectively; $F = 7.78$, df $= 1, 87$, $p < 0.01$). There were no significant interactions between conditions. These main effects were later replicated in an analysis of covariance in which the degree of cost involved in helping was partialled out. Thus, differences in perceived obligation to help cannot be accounted for simply by reference to differential costs involved in helping.

The first finding, that serious situations carry a stronger obligation to help, is both intuitive and consistent with past research. Studies reviewed by Staub (1978, pp. 225–241) indicate that helping is more likely to occur when the recipient's need for help and dependence are high. Interviews with selected subjects revealed that people were mainly concerned with the gravity of the consequences for the victim if help was not given. A slightly different slant was offered by respondents who stated that if they failed to help in a serious situation, they would feel guilty. According to these respondents, in failing to alleviate the extreme distress of another person, the non-helper becomes partially responsible for the further suffering of the victim. This interpretation supports Rosenhan's assertion that helping behaviour is often motivated by self-imposed sanctions (Rosenhan, 1978).

With regard to the doing versus giving distinction, Eric Fromm (1957:20–21) once noted that people regard the giving of oneself as being a higher good than the giving of one's possessions. The respondents seemed to agree. Generally, respondents reported that in many circumstances giving things to people can be awkward, superficial, or even vulgar. Doing things for people was seen as being much more positive. The research of Gergen and his associates (Gergen, Ellsworth, Maslach and Seipel, 1975) may be relevant here. This study, replicated in three countries, indicated that people do not generally like receiving "donations", especially if it is difficult to reciprocate. This appears to be true even if the recipient has a clear need for material assistance. Giving can highlight the recipient's dependent status, perhaps even leading to lowered self-esteem and lowered perceived competence. Furthermore, it can create an onerous feeling of obligation on the part of the recipient. On the other hand, doing things for people seems to more often imply getting involved with others on a more equal, co-operative level. Doing forms of helping are likely to be easier to reciprocate as well.

Respondents stressed the more personal nature of "doing" forms of helping. Some stated that doing, as opposed to giving, allows the helper to share more in the experience and perhaps achieve a feeling of accomplishment at having done something useful. Other respondents stressed a different aspect of doing and giving: in giving, the donor loses control over his resources, with the choice of how they are going to be utilized being left up to the recipient. With doing forms of help, however, the helper exercises control over the nature of the benefit to the recipient. In this way, he or she is more able to ensure that the investment is "well spent".

The finding that anonymous help carries a greater obligation than personal help appears counter-intuitive. Yet, the reasons respondents gave for rating the situations in this way are compelling. First, when people are giving personal kinds of assistance (assistance which is usually given to a friend), the reasons why help is given have less to do with the perception of a strong moral obligation than they do with the fact that people simply want to help. Thus, it seems likely that personal forms of helping result more from empathic processes than they do from internalized standards of behaviour. On the other hand, anonymous forms of help-giving usually occur in situations where empathy is less likely to guide behaviour, with prosocial activities being more under the guidance of social and personal norms.

A number of other reasons were offered for this tendency as well. If the type of helping in question is very personal, like comforting someone who has lost a loved one, there is a certain hesitancy to intrude lest you violate the other person's privacy. With intimate problems, people may not always wish to be helped, and rushing in before someone is ready might do more harm than good. Another reason given was that the obligation to help friends is less strong because there are fewer time constraints involved. Unless the problem is really urgent, you can usually help a friend at some future time. However, with a stranger, or a person seen infrequently, help must generally be given on the spot or not at all. Finally, it is often easier to say "no" to a friend than a stranger for a friend may be more sympathetic to your reasons for not getting involved and be less likely to think badly of you for failing to help. Strangers, however, can put you on the spot in ways which are difficult to avoid.

While some of these perceptions may be specific to the Australian sample studied, the results for the personal–anonymous distinction are consistent with the findings from an American survey conducted by Schreiber and Glidewell (1978). In this research it was found that in a sample of respondents (who were all currently receiving help from a friend or family member), only 56 percent believed they had an explicit right to ask for and receive help from friends and family. However, 73 percent believed they had an explicit right to ask for and receive help from a professional source (like a counsellor).

Question 2, dealing with people's perceptions of how most people would behave, and question 3, dealing with people's expectations about their own behaviour, yielded very similar results. For question 2, the analysis of variance resulted in a significant main effect for planned–spontaneous ($F = 11.85$, df $= 1, 87$, $p = 0.001$) and a significant interaction, between planned–spontaneous and personal–anonymous ($F = 5.195$, df $= 1, 87$, $p = 0.025$). The analysis of variance on question 3 also yielded a marginally significant main effect for planned–spontaneous ($F = 2.85$, df $= 1, 87$, $p = <0.10$) and a significant interaction between planned–spontaneous and personal–anonymous ($F = 7.35$, df $= 1, 87$, $p < 0.01$). The main effects indicate that for both people's expectations about the behaviour of themselves and others, spontaneous help is seen as being much more likely to be given than is planned help.

The interaction was nearly identical for both questions, so only the data from question 2 will be presented. These data, displayed in Table 6.3 and Figure 6.4, reveal that under planned conditions, personal forms of help were more likely to be given, while under spontaneous conditions anonymous forms of help were more likely to be given. Another way of describing the data is to say that personal help is given to about the same degree regardless of whether the situation is planned ahead of time or spontaneous. However, anonymous help is very likely to be given under spontaneous conditions but is very unlikely to be given if it requires planning. Both this effect and the main effects were later replicated for both questions using an analysis of covariance with cost as a covariate. Thus, these expectations of behaviour cannot be accounted for by referring to the amount of cost involved.

TABLE 6.3   *Mean expectation that most people would help in planned versus spontaneous and personal versus anonymous episodes[1]*

	Spontaneous	Planned
Personal	4.12 (SD = 0.96) (n = 24)	3.78 (SD = 1.12) (n = 27)
Anonymous	4.48 (SD = 1.29) (n = 28)	3.26 (SD = 1.05) (n = 24)

[1] Helping expectations range from 1 to 7 with a high number indicating most people would offer to help.

In contrast, this interaction effect was completely non-existent for the moral-obligation question ($F = 0.047$). Subjects regarded planned–anonymous forms of helping as carrying just as great an obligation to help as any other kind. However, the respondents pointed out that even though planned–anonymous helping often involves "good causes" certain characteristics of these situations make them problematic as far as actual involvement is concerned. For one thing, planned–anonymous forms of helping (such as giving money to a charity, volunteering for a psychology experiment, passing out leaflets for a social cause or political campaign, etc.) often have little immediacy, with the recipient being distant in both time and space. Since help does not have to be given right away, it can be put off, perhaps indefinitely. Because it is often the case that no one is watching, these situations tend to be easy to avoid. It may also be easy to rationalize one's failure to get involved. For example, it is often the case that other potential helpers are available, making it easier for any one person to think "someone else will do it" or ask "why should I be the one?". One could also reason that these kinds of helping require volunteers with special characteristics, like being wealthy (in contributing money to charities) or not being easily embarrassed (in going from door to door soliciting contributions), or being a good listener (in answering phones for an organization). Respondents also noted that anonymous forms of help-giving tend to have little to offer the helper. Because the helper is less likely to be involved in an ongoing relationship with the recipient, he may not get to see the product of his labour, especially if it involves helping at a distance.

However, the pattern is quite different if an individual is suddenly

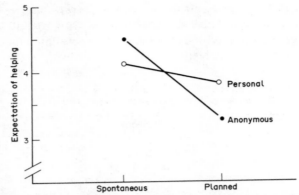

F<small>IG.</small> 6.4   Mean expectation that most other people would help in planned versus spontaneous and personal versus anonymous episodes.

confronted with a spontaneous situation where anonymous help is needed. Since the recipient's need is immediate, the situation has greater salience for the helper. The recipient may also be physically present, making it difficult to avoid him or her. Because the potential helper is already in the situation, it may be very difficult to back out or ignore it. Thus, the individual experiences a number of situational constraints which make anonymous help-giving more likely.

It is instructive to compare the results of questions 2 and 3, regarding expectations of behaviour for self and others, with the actual frequencies of different types of help reported in the preceding section of this chapter. As stated earlier, the greater frequency of non-serious as opposed to serious help, and personal as opposed to anonymous help, is probably a reflection of the fact that these types of situations are simply more likely to occur in everyday interaction. Thus, one would not necessarily expect these differences in rates to be paralleled in the normative questionnaire data. Other parallels, however, should be apparent if there is any consistency between what people say they and others would do and what, in fact, most people actually do in the way of everyday helping.

This appears to be the case. First, consistent with the subject's expectations in the questionnaire role-playing data, there were fewer reported behavioural incidents of planned help than anonymous help. Second, the same interaction effect between planned–spontaneous and personal–anonymous helping in the questionnaire data was apparent in the behavioural data as well. As reported in the previous section, personal forms of helping were only slightly more likely to be spontaneous than planned, while anonymous forms of helping were overwhelmingly spontaneous. Planned, anonymous helping incidents were very rare. Also, it can be recalled that the frequency of doing forms of helping was higher than the frequency of giving forms of helping (60 percent vs. 40 percent). There was a tendency for this to be reflected in the questionnaire data as well: subjects reported that they would be more likely to engage in doing than giving forms of helping at a marginal significance level ($F = 3.32$, $df = 1, 87, p = 0.07$). Overall, there appears to be a considerable amount of consistency between the kinds of helping behaviour people report engaging in during everyday interaction and their normative expectations about what others, and they themselves, would do in hypothetical situations.

It is argued here that there is consistency for two reasons. First, the linkage between expectations of behaviour and actual behaviour is examined in relation to everyday behaviour in naturalistic settings rather than manipulated behaviour in artificial laboratory situations. Secondly, the classification of variables is derived from people's own implicit understanding of helping. The researchers have not imposed their own categories of behaviour on the research subjects. Instead, naturally occurring behaviour is being viewed from the point of view of the actors themselves. Thus, it is not surprising that this type of approach yields consistency when some other approaches have not.

Before concluding this discussion, one more aspect of the data will be considered. This concerns the relating of background characteristics of people to various types of helping. Previous research has shown that people have preferences for alternative types of helping (Gergen, Gergen and Meter, 1972; Staub, 1974). Is it possible to relate certain "types" of people to preferences for helping forms in different regions of the multidimensional helping space?

As a first step to answering this question, the subjects in this study were divided into two groups: those majoring in a helping profession (social work or clinical psychology) and those majoring in non-helping professions (commerce, natural sciences, etc.). A few students were not sure, or did not report their major, and had to be omitted from the analysis. The choice of going into a helping as opposed to a non-helping profession was conceptualized as a major life-decision reflecting an entire set of attitudes, values and beliefs about helping. It was expected that people working towards careers in the helping professions would display patterns of expectations about the types of help they would be likely to engage in compared to other students.

To test this idea, a $2 \times 2 \times 2 \times 2 \times 2$ analysis of variance was conducted on the questionnaire item dealing with expectations of helping. The first four factors were the same as the ones used earlier, with helping versus non-helping profession forming the fifth factor. Because the sample size was small for such a large number of factors, all four- and five-way interactions were ignored and the sums of squares were pooled into the error term, thus ensuring that all cells on which a significant interaction was based contained at least six cases.

For this questionnaire item, the amount of variance accounted for increased substantially from 19 percent without the career variable to 45 percent with the career variable. In the analysis of variance with the career variable included, the first four factors and their interactions accounted for 21 percent of the variance, the career choice factor accounted for 2 percent of the variance, and the interactions between the career choice factor and the helping episode factors accounted for 21 percent of the variance. While the main effect for the career choice variable was not significant ($F = 2.1$, $df = 1, 66$, $p > 0.10$), indicating that helping majors reported being no more likely to offer help overall, there were three significant interactions involving this factor. First, there was a three-way interaction between helping–non-helping major, spontaneous–planned, and personal–anonymous ($F = 7.62$, $df = 1, 66$, $p < 0.01$). These data appear in Figure 6.5. Inspection of the cell means reveals that when the type of help is spontaneously given, both helping majors and non-helping majors reported that they would be more likely to give anonymous help than personal help, to about the same degree. However, when the type of help was planned ahead of time, helping majors indicated a clear preference for planned–personal forms of helping, the type of helping which was rated at least likely by the non-helping majors.

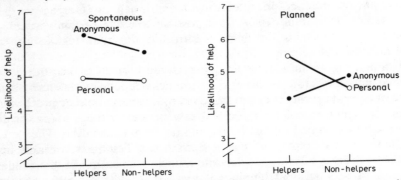

FIG. 6.5 Mean reported likelihood of helping in planned versus spontaneous and personal versus anonymous episodes, for subjects majoring in helping and non-helping professions.

Second, there was a significant three-way interaction between helping–non-helping majors, personal–anonymous, and giving–doing ($F = 11.78$, $df = 1, 66$, $p = 0.001$). Inspection of the cell means indicated that when the situation required giving, helpers and non-helpers reported being equally likely to help, regardless of whether help was given personally or anonymously. However, when the situation required doing forms of assistance, helping majors reported being more likely to help under

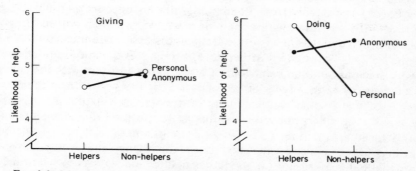

Fig. 6.6   Mean reported likelihood of helping in giving versus doing and personal versus anonymous episodes, for subjects majoring in helping and non-helping professions.

The third interaction involved helping versus non-helping major, planned–spontaneous, and giving–doing ($F = 10.26$, $df = 1, 66$, $p < 0.01$). The interpretation of this interaction appears to be that non-helping majors preferred spontaneous to planned giving while helping majors preferred planned to spontaneous giving.

Overall, these data indicate that, in comparison to students majoring in non-helping fields, students studying social work and clinical psychology have a clear preference for planned–personal, personal–doing and planned–giving forms of helping. The first two types of helping are consistent with the kinds of helping activities one would expect social workers and clinical psychologists to be involved in on a professional basis. Thus, there appears to be a parallel between the kinds of helping people reported being likely to engage in and their decision to enter career fields which involve these same forms of helping.

The amount of cost item was also used as a dependent variable in a similar $2 \times 2 \times 2 \times 2 \times 2$ analysis of variance to see if people planning helping careers were different to others in the amount of cost they associated with various types of helping. Briefly, the results of this procedure indicated that helping majors rated planned–personal forms of helping as less costly, and planned–anonymous forms of helping as more costly than did non-helping majors ($F = 6.70$, $df = 1, 66$, $p = <0.01$). Helping majors also rated personal–doing forms of helping as being less costly than anonymous–doing forms of helping while non-helping majors rated personal–doing forms of helping as being more costly than anonymous–doing forms of helping ($F = 5.45$, $df = 1, 66$, $p < 0.05$). These findings are consistent with the previous ones, and suggest that people going into helping professions prefer personal–doing and planned–person al forms of helping because they enjoy them more and find them less difficult than do people aiming for careers in non-helping fields.

Although these results are preliminary, they are encouraging. It appears that people's expectations of their own behaviour, their perceptions of social norms, and their own personal standards of behaviour can be related to the helping taxonomy. Furthermore, people's expectations about their own behaviour, and the behaviour of others, are consistent with the actual frequencies of various types of helping which people report from everyday life. Finally, personal characteristics of people, such as the choice of a career in a helping profession, can be related to preferences for helping forms located in certain regions of the multidimensional helping space. Further implications of the taxonomy for theory and research into prosocial behaviour, and for the larger field of social psychology, will be taken up in Chapter 7.

7

New Directions for Theory and Research

P. R. AMATO, M. SMITHSON and P. PEARCE

Implications of the Helping Taxonomy for Theory and Research

AN OBVIOUS organizing advantage of a taxonomy, in any field of inquiry, is that it allows researchers to establish the range and limitations of theoretical and empirical generalizations. Yet, while the development of empirically derived classificatory schemes has been a major preliminary step in the natural sciences like chemistry and biology, this activity has received little attention in many areas of social psychology. This may be partially due to the fact that social psychology has modelled itself more after the parametric sciences than the structural sciences (Backman, 1979). The absence of taxonomic concerns may also be due to the greater difficulty inherent in classifying social behaviours, which are dependent upon the definitions of social actors for their meanings, as compared to the physical, more "objective" subject matter of the natural sciences. Thus, while it is a relatively straightforward task to cluster the phenotypic characteristics of living organisms into their basic types, it is a more difficult problem to identify the salient underlying structural similarities in social behaviours. The relatively recent development of rigorous, descriptive quantitative techniques like multidimensional scaling and the availability of computer packages to implement them has probably led to an increased interest in this type of research activity in social psychology.

The need for a taxonomic classification of one's subject matter to guide theory and research seems obvious. Intuitively, it is apparent that the kind of help given when intervening in emergencies is different from the kind of help given when donating money to charities, providing emotional support to friends and family, or doing small favours for strangers. Yet, social psychologists have persisted in referring to all of these behaviours, and more, as "helping" and have continued to make the decision quite arbitrarily as to which kind of helping to include in their research. The result has been a large number of research pieces which examine the effect of some variable such as empathy on helping, but give no specification as to how empathy might be differently involved in one form of helping as opposed to another.

It is argued here that serious attention to the perceived characteristics of helping types would allow researchers to make more precise generalizations about the factors involved in helping processes. This would result in a contingency model of helping in which certain processes and variables are held to be relevant for helping episodes lying in one region of the taxonomy but are less relevant for helping episodes lying in other regions. It is anticipated that explanations for helping may differ substantially as one considers the full range of helping types. In this section three implications of this "meta-theoretical" contingency model will be discussed. These involve (1) establishing the perimeters of theoretical generalizations and the delineation of "relevancy domains" for classes of variables, (2) comparing the results of separate empirical studies and resolving apparent contradictions in the literature, (3) consideration of the interaction between personal characteristics and helping-episode characteristics.

Theoretical Generalizations and the Helping Taxonomy

In Chapter 1, four general theories which have been applied to prosocial behaviour were briefly reviewed. While each of these theories has been shown to have explanatory power for some aspects of helping, no single theory can account for all, or even most, of the empirical findings in this area. There is nothing surprising in this, as no field of study in the psychological or social sciences possesses anything resembling the theoretical integration provided by Newton's three laws of motion or Darwin's Evolution of Species, or is likely to in the foreseeable future. Nevertheless, there is a certain lack of clarity in the field of helping because each theory fails to specify the range of activities for which its explanations are expected to hold. The result is the existence of a number of theories with unknown domains of relevancy and validity.

In the case of attribution theory, research done within this framework indicates that the inferences individuals make about the cause of another's dependency affect the likelihood of offering help. According to Weiner (1980), attributing the cause to uncontrollable factors increases the amount of sympathy experienced for the victim which in turn leads to a greater probability of help being given. Like most theories, this formulation is assumed to hold good for a large range of helping episodes. His comment, "The model outlined . . . is expected to generalize across a variety of help-giving situations" (p. 197) is typical of much theoretical writing. But how can this "variety of help-giving situations" be established? What is required is some sort of organizing model to guide the choice of replication contexts.

It is likely that there are many situations in which knowing the cause of another's dependency is not relevant to the decision to offer help. Consider the seriousness and personalness dimensions of the helping taxonomy. It could be hypothesized that attribution processes are most salient when seriousness is low or moderate, and less salient when seriousness is high. For example, when someone's life is in danger, a bystander's inference that the victim is responsible for his own misfortune, and the negative evaluation this entails, are likely to be over-ridden by sympathetic concern for the victim's extreme suffering or the conviction of the bystanders personally held norms. Likewise, intimate help given to a loved one may be more resistant to attribution effects than anonymous help given to strangers.

To test this notion, a small-scale questionnaire study was carried out, similar to the one reported in Weiner (1980). In the present study, subjects read short written descriptions of episodes in which a person is in need and made judgements about the likelihood that they would help. The first stage of this research used the same situation reported in Weiner (1980) and dealt with a person (described as being either ill or drunk) collapsing in public. Seventy-two student volunteers read either the "drunk" or the "ill" version and gave their reactions on a number of 9-point bipolar scales. The results essentially replicated those of Weiner. Subjects rated the drunk victim as being significantly more responsible for his predicament ($F = 24.48$, $df = 1, 70$, $p < 0.001$), reported feeling less sympathy for the drunk ($F = 5.48$, $df = 1, 70$, $p < 0.05$) and reported being less likely to help the drunk ($F = 13.92$, $df = 1, 70$, $p < 0.001$). Correlational analysis also revealed that ratings of the victim's responsibility were negatively correlated with helping judgements ($r = -0.42$, $p < 0.001$) and ratings of sympathy were positively correlated with helping judgements ($r = 0.59$, $p < 0.001$). However, subjects also rated the drunk victim as being much more costly to help ($F = 13.8$, $df = 1, 70$, $p < 0.001$), indicating that cost (a variable not included in the Weiner study) was confounded with controllability.

Due to the non-comparability of the "drunk" and "ill" episodes, it was decided to use another kind of helping situation in the present research. The situation used was based upon an automobile accident which was said to be due to either the victim's reckless driving (controllable) or an accidental blow-out (uncontrollable) and in which the driver was either badly hurt (serious) or not hurt (not serious). The situation is given below:

You are walking along the street in a residential area when an automobile comes round the corner. The driver is driving fast in a reckless manner and the automobile skids and hits a telephone pole (the driver is driving slowly and carefully but the automobile has a blow-out and skids into a telephone pole). The driver is badly hurt, bleeding and barely conscious. S/he asks you if you could call an ambulance (the driver is not hurt and gets out of the car to inspect the damage. S/he asks you if you could call a friend) from the public telephone which is just up the street from you.

The two factors of controllability and seriousness were counterbalanced in a 2 × 2 factorial design. Fifty-two university student volunteers read one of the four versions and gave their reactions on a number of 9-point bipolar scales. A manipulation check revealed that subjects rated the "serious" accident as being more serious than the "nonserious" accident (means were, respectively, 7.37 and 3.62; $t = 5.78$, d$f = 1, 50$, $p < 0.001$), and the driver in the controllable situation was rated as being more responsible for his predicament than the driver in the "uncontrollable" situation (means were, respectively, 6.62 and 2.73; $t = 5.31$, d$f = 1, 50$, $p < 0.001$). Perceived cost of helping was not related to either the controllability or seriousness manipulation ($p > .1$).

The mean ratings on the likelihood of helping scale for the four cells in the design are displayed in Table 7.1. A 2 × 2 analysis of variance revealed a main effect for controllability ($F = 11.54$, d$f = 1, 48$, $p < 0.001$) and a main effect for seriousness ($F = 4.98$, d$f = 1, 48$, $p < 0.05$). While the interaction was not significant ($F = 2.12$, d$f = 1, 48$, $p > 0.1$), inspection of the means indicates that the effect of controllability was pronounced in the low seriousness condition, but was very slight in the high seriousness condition. Post-hoc analysis revealed that the mean for the non-serious–controllable condition was significantly different from all other means, with no other differences between means being significant. Thus, the interpretation of these results would appear to be that helping judgements were generally very high, except when the victim was responsible for his predicament and when the situation was not serious.

TABLE 7.1 *Mean helping judgement under controllable versus uncontrollable and non-serious versus serious conditions[1]*

		Non-serious accident	Serious accident
Uncontrollable	Mean	8.38[2]	8.69
	SD	(0.77)	(0.63)
Controllable	Mean	6.46	7.92
	SD	(1.76)	(2.02)

[1] Helping judgements range from 1 to 9 with high numbers indicating a high likelihood of helping.
[2] The n for each cell is 13.

Correlational analysis also leads to the same conclusion (see Table 7.2). In the non-serious condition the predictions of attribution theory were strongly confirmed. Helping judgements were positively related to sympathy ($r = 0.54$, $p < 0.01$) and negatively related to attributed responsibility ($r = -0.61$, $p < 0.001$). Furthermore, sympathy was strongly negatively related to attributed responsibility ($r = -0.73$, $p < 0.001$). Multiple-regression analysis revealed that the variables sympathy and responsibility jointly accounted for 37 percent of the variance in helping ratings ($R = 0.62$, $p < 0.05$).

TABLE 7.2   *Correlation matrix for likelihood of helping, sympathy and victim, victim's responsibility, and perceived seriousness variable*[1]

	Likelihood of helping	Sympathy for victim	Victim's responsibility	Seriousness of accident
Likelihood of helping	—	0.54**	−0.61***	−0.05
Sympathy for victim	0.29	—	−0.73***	−0.09
Victim's responsibility	0.12	−0.45*	—	−0.03
Seriousness of accident	0.41*	0.18	0.17	—

[1] Upper half matrix contains correlations for the non-serious condition; lower half matrix contains correlations for the serious condition.
* $= p < 0.05$ ** $= p < 0.01$ *** $= p < 0.001$

However, in the serious condition, people's self-expectations of helping were no longer significantly related to either reported sympathy ($r = 0.29$, $p > 0.1$) or attributed responsibility ($r = 0.12$, $p > 0.1$). The decrease in association between likelihood of helping and attributed responsibility is statistically significant ($Z = 2.77$, $p < 0.01$). In this condition, perceived seriousness turned out to be the best predictor of helping judgements ($r = 0.41$, $p < 0.05$). Sympathy and responsibility, jointly, accounted for a non-significant 16 percent of the variance ($R = 0.40, p > 0.1$), a substantial decrease from the previous condition.

The results of this research indicate that the predictions of attribution theory may be more appropriate for certain kinds of helping situations than others. While the general pattern of Weiner's (1980) results were replicated with the "drunk" and "ill" situations borrowed from his study, and with a non-serious automobile accident situation, the predicted relationship between controllability and helping judgements did not appear in a serious-automobile-accident situation. Discussions with subjects suggested that even though the victim was perceived as being responsible for the accident, and even though there was little sympathy generated by the victim's distress, subjects felt they simply had to intervene. To have failed to provide aid under such serious circumstances would have gone against most people's moral standards. Thus, personal helping norms probably account for the behaviour of subjects in this condition better than attribution theory's emphasis upon the inferences people make about the causes of the victim's distress. Further research may be able to delineate those types of helping for which casual attributions are most relevant in explaining helping behaviour.

The results of this study are consistent with those of a pilot study reported by Staub (1978, p. 235) in which equivalent levels of help were given to a person regardless of whether the victim's distress was self-induced or not. Staub argued that when a person's distress is severe, people frequently disregard information about its source in responding to it.

A taxonomy can offer similar organizing advantages to other theories as well. In regard to social-learning theory, it is likely that observational and modelling processes are important in learning a wide range of helping behaviours. However, a problem in this area concerns the extent of stimulus generalization from one type of helping situation to the next. For example, one study (Elliot and Vasta, 1970) showed that modelled sharing behaviour generalized from a sharing-candy situation to one in which children had the opportunity to share pennies. However, research by Weissbrod (1976) indicates that learning to donate resources does not generalize to rescuing behaviour. It is argued here that the extent to which individuals will generalize, or discriminate between, situations will depend upon how they define and categorize helping episodes. The extent of stimulus generalization, or discrimination learning, will depend upon the closeness of these helping episodes in a cognitive, perceptual space. With a classificatory scheme of sufficient detail it might be possible to establish the "spread of effect" of specific learning experiences.

Likewise, equity theory predicts that individuals will feel obligated to reciprocate, on an equal basis, help which they have received from others. However, this normative expectation may breakdown in serious, emergency situations where other norms and motives over-ride those concerned with equity. Likewise, it is difficult to see how equity concerns could be relevant to people engaging in anonymous helping with complete strangers. Further, equity considerations may be less relevant in the very personal types of helping. Rubin (1973) indicates that people in close relationships often do not expect reciprocation for positive acts because what benefits one person benefits the other as well. Likewise, research with children suggests that reciprocity concerns are less salient in interactions between good friends (Staub, 1978:369). Other research indicates that there is a high level of reciprocity between strangers in regard to levels of self-disclosure in interaction, but little immediate reciprocity between friends (Derlega *et al.*, 1976). Thus, predictions based on equity theory may hold only for the middle range of the personal–anonymous continuum.

With regard to cognitive-development theory, it would be important to know if the use of moral rules can vary depending upon the kind of help in question. Research indicates that people do not consistently operate with the same set of rules at all times (Staub, 1979). It appears that situational forces can change the level of moral reasoning used. Levine (1976) found that the level of moral reasoning used varied with the identity of the person in need: stranger, family, or friend. Research by Eisenberg-Berg and Neal (1981) suggests that certain situational conditions such as the degree of cost involved in helping can affect the nature of children's moral reasoning. Therefore, it may be that some people apply one set of rules (for example, those concerned with doing one's duty) when it comes to donating money to charities, and another set of rules (involving notions of democratic rights, community responsibility and internalized standards) when giving assistance to friends and family.

Generally speaking, it is probably the case that theories, such as cognitive-development theory, which emphasize stable, intrapsychic structures, traits, or abilities have greater salience for forms of helping which are planned rather than spontaneous. In completely spontaneous situations, the individual may be forced to make a decision very quickly. Often these situations involve strangers or events which are unfamiliar to the individual. In highly ambiguous situations like these, it is not likely that individuals will have time to assess their beliefs and values or consider the match between their own personalities and abilities and the help required. Instead, the individual is more likely to rely upon situational cues such as the behaviour of others, the ambiguity of the situation, or the individual's own mood in deciding whether to give assistance.

However, with planned forms of prosocial behaviour, there is less immediacy involved, allowing the individual time to think over and consider all the implications of helping. Since the individual is "at a distance" from the helping situation, it is unlikely that situational variables will be of much salience. Instead, the individual's decision will more likely reflect his or her values, personally held standards, preferences and personality. Thus, situational variables should be of more importance in spontaneous helping situations and stable, intrapsychic variables should be of more importance in planned helping situations (Benson et al., 1980).

There is support for this distinction in the helping literature. A large number of studies which used spontaneous forms of helping have failed to find dispositional correlates of helping (cf. Darley and Batson, 1973). However, studies investigating planned forms of helping have often found just such correlations (Benson, et al., 1980; Schwartz, 1977; Pomazal and Jaccard, 1976; London, 1970; Rosenhan, 1970). Nevertheless, the helping literature tends to give the impression that situational variables are more important in explaining helping behaviour than are stable, intrapsychic variables. This, however, is probably a reflection of the fact that the majority of published studies have used spontaneous help-giving situations. Within a laboratory-based experimental paradigm, spontaneous forms of helping are simply easier to simulate and study than are planned forms of helping. Indeed, all of the studies of planned help-giving mentioned above which found personal correlates of helping relied upon questionnaire or interview methods. Thus, the pattern which emerges from these considerations is that social psychologists, through their commitment to an experimental methodology, have mainly limited themselves to the study of spontaneous forms of helping, with the result being that situational variables are widely held to be more important in explaining helping responses than are dispositional variables. However, the research presented in Chapter 6 indicates that planned forms of helping are quite common in everyday life. Thus, personal characteristics of individuals are probably more important in understanding everyday helping than laboratory-bound research would lead us to believe.

These considerations suggest that entire classes of variables may have limited domains of relevancy. Another example of this notion refers to people's underlying motivations for helping. Rushton (1980) has suggested that the range of motivations to engage in altruistic behaviour can be subsumed under two basic motivational systems: empathy and personal norms of helping. In Chapter 6 it was reported that respondents stated a stronger moral obligation to give anonymous help to strangers than to give personal help to friends. The reason for this finding was postulated to be that personal forms of helping between friends are more likely to be guided by empathic processes while anonymous forms of helping between strangers are more likely to be guided by personal norms and internalized standards of behaviour. Research evidence indicates that attitudinal similarity increases the likelihood of empathy, and hence, prosocial behaviour (Krebs, 1975) and that positive experiences with, and attraction for, another person can increase prosocial behaviour (Kelley and Byrne, 1976). Furthermore, Hornstein (1972, 1978) has theorized that similarity and liking for another person increase "promotive tension" or the empathic identification with another's needs and goals. It is apparent that liking, similarity and the sharing of positive experiences are more likely to exist between friends than between strangers. Hence, the conditions conducive to empathically mediated helping are more likely to exist in the personal, ongoing relationships between friends than in the anonymous, transitory encounters between strangers. In the absence of empathy, one might still be motivated to give anonymous forms of assistance (like donating blood, giving someone directions, or donating to charities) by a sense of community responsibility, a belief in the correctness of aiding dependent others, or a perceived obligation to do one's duty.

In summary, the eventual development of a contingency model of helping behaviour in which certain classes of variables and types of explanations are systematically related to certain categories of helping would seem a desirable direction in which to move. It may turn out that certain variables or theories are more general in that they have relevance for a wide range of helping situations. Others may turn out to be quite narrow in focus. Nevertheless, the accuracy of predictions about behaviour in specific situations would be improved by taking into consideration the nature of the helping episode and its place in the taxonomic scheme. Such a procedure would be comparable to that which exists in many other scientific fields of study.

Comparing the Results of Studies and Resolving Inconsistencies

Social psychologists have been aware of the difficulty in generalizing research findings across qualitatively different types of helping. For example, Bar-tal (1976) claims that emergency and non-emergency situations arouse different social norms, motives and hence response sets (p. 51). However, while the distinction between emergency and non-emergency types of helping is an obvious one, researchers have largely been in the dark regarding the salient distinguishing features of most other forms of helping, and hence, the degree to which they can be meaningfully compared.

Lack of attention to the qualitative differences between different forms of helping has probably led to a number of apparently contradictory findings in the literature. One example would be the findings regarding sex differences. While a large number of studies have found no differences between males and females in rates of helping, a number of other studies have found just such differences. As Bar-tal has suggested, "A possible explanation for this discrepancy lies in the nature of the required act of help manipulated in the studies" (p. 61). A search through the literature reveals that studies reporting significantly higher rates of helping for males than females have used the following measures of helping: calling a garage (Gaertner and Bickman, 1971), picking up a hitchhiker (Pomazal and Clore, 1973), picking up fallen groceries (Wispé and Freshley, 1971), giving change (Raymond and Unger, 1972), helping someone with a stuck shopping cart (Harris and Bays, 1973), picking up fallen pencils (Latané and Dabbs, 1975), picking up a dropped package (Page, 1977), fixing a flat tyre (Bryan and Test, 1967; West, Whitney and Schnedler, 1975), giving direct assistance to an epileptic (Schwartz and Clausen, 1970; Darley and Latané, 1968), assisting a collapsed person on the subway (Piliavin, Rodin and Piliavin, 1969; Piliavin and Piliavin, 1972), driving a stranger in distress to his home (Shotland and Huston, 1979), and helping someone carry a big armload of heavy boxes (Rudestam, 1976).

All of these situations involve active, doing, spontaneous, anonymous forms of assistance. This trend is reinforced by an analysis of archival data undertaken by Lay, Allen and Kassirer (1974). They found that out of the 101 recipients of the Carnegie Hero Medal for 1971, 96 were male. The situations in which these acts of bravery occurred could be classified as above, that is, as active, doing, spontaneous, and anonymous (drowning situations, burning buildings or automobiles, etc.). Furthermore, in an analysis of Toronto Civilian Citation Recipients, 108 out of the 147 people receiving citations for "spontaneous service to citizens in aiding the police force" for a 3-year period were male (73 percent). Of the 39 females awarded citations, 23 percent had engaged in direct intervention of some sort in a crime situation. The comparable figure for direct intervention for males was 61 percent (Lay, Allen and Kassirer, 1974). This is further supported in a study by Huston *et al.* (1981) in which intervenors claiming compensation under California's Good Samaritan statute were interviewed. Out of 32 individuals studied who had intervened at the scene of an ongoing crime, 31 were male.

Only a small number of studies in the helping literature report higher rates of helping for females. These studies used forms of helping which were more planned, formal, personal and less likely to involve direct intervention. These include donating to a charity (Nadler, Romek and Shapiro-Friedman, 1979), yielding to a dependent partner in a simulation game (Schopler and Bateson, 1965), helping a dependent fellow worker in a simulated-work situation (Berkowitz, 1969) and helping a younger child with a difficult task (O'Bryant and Brophy, 1976). The fact that these studies are few in number reflects, of course, the tendency for social psychologists to neglect the study of planned and personal helping. Furthermore, research reviewed by Staub (1978, chap. 4) indicates that females are likely to favour themselves less than males when distributing rewards they have earned. Other studies have found female students rated higher on "service" (Hartshorne, May and Maller, 1929), considerateness and social responsibility (Bronfenbrenner, 1961). A variety of studies indicate that females score higher on empathy measures than males (Hoffman, 1977). Finally, Staub (1978) in his review of sex differences in helping concludes "The results with both children and adults suggest that considerations for others is a more salient and important value for females than for males" (p. 257).

Thus, it may be that situations which elicit spontaneous, anonymous, active, doing forms of assistance (such as emergency intervention, providing physical help, etc.) may activate a norm which is more salient for males than for females. Females, however, may be more attuned to situations which require planned, personal, sharing forms of assistance (sharing possessions, providing emotional support and comfort, etc.). This might reflect different perceived competencies resulting from the differential sex-role socialization patterns of our culture.

This suggestion regarding sex differences is somewhat speculative, but the basic idea could be tested by presenting males and females with a variety of helping situations and then comparing rates of help-giving between sexes across the situations. Ideally, information on sex-role internalization should be included. However, the point of the example is to suggest that before the results of studies can be meaningfully compared, the nature of the helping task must be taken into account. Apparently contradictory findings may turn out to be less contradictory than imagined if the helping situations used have very different characteristics. Also, the example regarding sex differences suggests that different groups of individuals may have preferences for different forms of help-giving. This point leads to a consideration of the problem of specifying person by situation interactions.

Interactions between Personal and Helping Episode Characteristics

Another area in which the present model may prove useful is in the search for personal variables relevant to helping. Some approaches, such as that of Pomazal and Jaccard (1976), imply that an individual's beliefs, values, motivations and normative expectations about certain types of helping can be strong predictors of helping behaviour, but only when the type of helping is narrowly specified (e.g. donating blood). This contrasts with other investigators (Schwartz, 1977; Rushton, 1980; Staub, 1974) who have tried to find personality traits which predict helping behaviour across wide varieties of situations.

The present model suggests a middle-range approach, one which recognizes that personal characteristics (such as personal norms, prosocial values and personality traits) may predict behaviour in certain regions of the multidimensional space but not in others.

Some research suggests that individuals have preferences for certain types of helping (Gergen, Gergen and Meter, 1972). Data presented in Chapter 6 indicate that people intending to have careers in the helping professions of social work and clinical psychology have preferences for planned–personal and personal–doing forms of helping. This notion is consistent with Staub's (1978) position regarding the activating potential of situations for personal, prosocial goals. Staub argues that a person's behaviour in a particular situation is a function of both the goals which the person holds and the extent to which a given situation activates these goals. As he states:

> ... even if certain people have similar goals, the range of applicability of their goals can vary. For example, some people may apply their concern about other's welfare only when physical need is involved. ... We have to develop measurement devices that will determine not only the existence and intensity of various personal goals but also the specific ranges in which they are applicable (p. 47).

A helping taxonomy like the present one may be useful in specifying the ranges of situations in which a person's prosocial goals, personal standards, perceived competencies, values, or personality might lead to helping. For example, some people may be eager to help family and friends in personal or intimate situations, but feel little compulsion to provide anonymous help to strangers. Likewise, others may be quite helpful in day-to-day situations and yet feel that it is best not to become involved in emergency situations. Some people are continually involved in formal, planned, organizational forms of helping while others avoid this kind of involvement. If the cognitively based taxonomy presented in this volume has isolated salient characteristics which people use to classify helping episodes, then it should aid in finding the ranges within which people's prosocial concerns and tendencies are likely to operate. This line of thought is consistent with past research which indicates that behavioural consistency is usually found only across very similar situations (Mischel, 1968). Of course, the extent of similarity is a question which must be decided by the actor, not the observer.

In summary, the approach advocated here is broadly consistent with the concern voiced in social psychology during the 1970s for studying person by situation interactions (Alker, 1972; Bowers, 1973; Ekehammar, 1974; Staub, 1978; Forgas, 1980). As Forgas (1980) has argued, combining measures of individuals, such as scores on personality scales, with measures of social episodes (on implicit cognitive dimension), will give better explanations and predictions than if only one or the other measure were used. By using a taxonomic scheme like the one presented in this volume, researchers can match characteristics of persons with characteristics of helping episodes to increase the amount of variance accounted for in behaviour. Such a procedure would be comparable to the example presented in Chapter 6 in which personal characteristics (helping versus non-helping profession) accounted for 2 percent of the variance, characteristics of the helping episode (planned versus spontaneous, etc.) accounted for 21 percent of the variance, and interactions between personal characteristics and helping episode characteristics accounted for 21 percent of the variance.

To conclude this section, it must be emphasized that although the helping taxonomy developed in this volume has shown a fair amount of stability across a number of studies and subject samples, it should not be considered a finished product. Data presented in Chapter 4 indicated that one or more salient cognitive dimensions used by subjects have yet to be satisfactorily labelled. Furthermore, the distinctions between planned and spontaneous help, personal and anonymous help, and so on, are very broad. It is highly likely that people also make more finely grained distinctions than these. For example, doing forms of helping might be further subdivided by some people into a number of types, as the Chapter 5 analysis suggested. The development of a more complete taxonomy, with perhaps more than one level of generality, must necessarily await the carrying out of further research. Ideally, this new research should be carried out with other cultural and national groups to establish the wider generality of the model.

The Potential for Applications

Results from the studies undertaken in Chapters 4 and 6 suggest some possible directions for applications of the social psychology of helping behaviour, especially in the areas of the helping professions and social welfare. This section, then, is devoted to a discussion of those possibilities, with the hope of stimulating further applied research and theory construction.

In Chapter 4, a comparison of people affiliated with the Liberal and Labour parties in North Queensland indicated that conservatives and progressives may think about helping, and therefore perhaps social welfare, in different ways. Liberals associate active intervention with high cost to a greater extent than Labourites, and the conservative view of helping may also cast help into an intervention (rather than donation) mould. If this result holds up under further empirical testing, then it raises several questions concerning the nature, of political ideology about social welfare.

First, the cognitive differences in the perception of helping provides a rival explanation for the origins of political differences in welfare policies. the traditional account of party differences places emphasis on values differences or conflicts of interest, with cognitive differences being epiphenomenal. Secondly, if the conflict between conservatives and progressives over the issue of community welfare is in part cognitively based, then conflict management and negotiation techniques may be required which differ widely from those used in values-based conflict. Some researchers have noted that the management of cognitively based conflict is a relatively underdeveloped area, but there is general recognition in the field that this kind of conflict is best dealt with by different strategies than those used for conventional kinds (e.g. Brehmer and Hammond, 1977).

The Chapter 6 study of helping-style preferences among various student samples indicated that helping profession-oriented students have markedly different preferences from those of their academic counterparts. The social work and clinical psychology students showed a preference for planned, personal intervention, which was least preferred by the non-helper students. These results lead to the question of what kinds of help the professional helper engages in while on the job, and whether that kind of helping occupies different regions in the general helping taxonomy than help given in everyday life.

The data collected for the Chapter 4 study comparing social-work students' and nurses' perceptions of everyday helping, on-the-job helping, and the hypothetical episodes used in this research, were reanalysed to investigate the above questions. The bipolar construct ratings were dichotomized to allow simple and direct comparisons with the distribution of everyday helping among the students studied in Chapter 6. The social-work students' everyday helping was virtually identically distributed as other students' everyday episodes, so these two samples were combined to form the "everyday" part of Table 7.3 below. The other subtables include the social-work students' and nurses' on-the-job helping in social work agency placements and at the hospital, respectively.

TABLE 7.3   *Frequencies of helping for professional helping and everyday helping (in percentages)*

		Planned		Spontaneous			
		Serious	Non-serious	Serious	Non-serious	Total	
Everyday	Doing	8	14	10	28	60	*(n = 474)*
	Giving	5	5	8	23	40	
Soc. work	Doing	52	6	16	5	79	*(n = 75)*
	Giving	8	7	5	1	21	
Nurses	Doing	30	18	3	22	73	*(n = 152*
	Giving	6	4	6	11	27	

The trend evident in this table is that the dominant style of social work and nursing helping is planned intervention in serious situations, a type of helping which is comparatively rare in everyday experience. This trend accords well with the Chapter 6 results concerning helping-style preferences expressed by helping-profession students, and it is unique to their job experiences since they do not appear to engage in this kind of help during ordinary daily life to any greater degree than nonhelper students. Table 7.4 shows a further breakdown of the social workers' and nurses' helping which reveals that these two groups tend to engage in planned intervention which is personal rather than anonymous.

While these findings may seem obvious to some readers, the mainstream literature on the helping professions nevertheless has largely overlooked the implications which follow from them. Many writers have claimed that professional helping is somehow special, especially in the methods and objectives involved. But few seem to have given serious thought to the fact that such help is unusual or even abnormal, insofar as it is of a kind rarely found in everyday life. Professional helping is planned, intervening, on a

TABLE 7.4   *Breakdown of helping frequencies for social workers and nurses (in percentages)*

			Planned		Spontaneous	
			Serious	Non-serious	Serious	Non-serious
Social workers	Personal	Doing	39	3	13	5
		Giving	7	4	5	1
	Anonymous	Doing	13	3	3	0
		Giving	1	3	0	0
Nurses	Personal	Doing	18	22	3	11
		Giving	4	2	6	11
	Anonymous	Doing	12	4	1	11
		Giving	1	2	0	0

personal level, often in serious or problematic situations, and yet it occurs between strangers. It is a kind of help, which, in addition to being rare, is also relatively unpreferred by people not involved in a helping profession. It is likely that this form of helping violates widely held social norms.

These propositions bear directly on such issues as the kind of person suited for helping professions, the sorts of social skills required for effectively gaining trust and rapport, and on the general problem of intervention effectiveness. The remainder of this section is devoted to an exploration of how the location of professional helping in the context of a general taxonomy of helping can provide insights into the effectiveness issue.

Much of the literature on the helping professional and intervention methods is centrally concerned with whether it works (see Briar, 1967, for a typical statement). Most schools of psychotheraphy and social work go through periods of self-doubt concerning effectiveness, and the recent swing in several countries toward evaluation reflects a heightened emphasis on finding out whether an intervention has been successful. Relatively little systematic work has been done, however, on those determinants of success which operate independently of intervention methods. Given the rather equivocal record of most social work and psycho-therapeutic methods to date, perhaps attention to such external influences is overdue.

The bulk of research which has attended to external influences on the success of intervention has focused on a search for the "effective helper" (in psychotherapy, see Carkhuff, 1969; Truax and Mitchell, 1971; and Egan, 1975). Studies in therapist effectiveness cumulated in the early 1970s with a consensus that the effective therapist is genuine or authentic, accurately empathic, and non-possessively warm (Truax and Mitchell, 1971:302). At about the same time, another line of research seemed to show that while some therapists do significantly better than either lay helpers or no treatment, other therapists actually do worse (Bergin and Garfield, 1971; Bergin, 1975). This difference was found both in individual and group therapy. Further, Bergin and his associates showed that some therapists worsen their clients' conditions through their attempts to help.

These findings indicate that some crucial information about the professional helper is missing. Why do the helping professions attract people who are unusually bad at helping as well as those who are adept? A clue might lie in the apparent preference of such people for planned personal intervention in serious or problematic situations. While there is a long-standing folk stereotype of the social worker or psychotherapist as a crusading secular messianic figure, little systematic work has been done regarding the expectations, motives and helping preferences of professionals. At least one writer (Smale, 1977) has proposed that expectations and self-fulfilling prophecies play an important part in therapeutic outcomes, but his treatment ignored the special nature of professional helping.

Another source of potential insight into the efficacy question is the investigation of the expectations, motives and values which clients bring to the helping situation. Surprisingly little attention has been devoted to this issue, except in the area of matching client and helping-professional values. Bloom (1975) comments that it is only as a "last resort" and with "considerable discomfort" that an individual with a problem becomes a client to a helping professional. However, this assertion was not supported with any empirical evidence. While recognizing that professional helping is unusual and counter-normative, and avoided by most people in everyday life, it may be instructive to ask about the conditions under which people are likely to seek or avoid that kind of help. There is clear room here for applied social psychological research into the client–helper relationship, in comparison with other kinds of helping.

Some General Implications of this Volume for Social Psychology

Methodological Issues

Attempts to organize an entire field of inquiry via empirically based taxonomies are comparatively rare, and the field of "meta-analysis", as some writers have chosen to call it (e.g. Glass, McGraw and Smith, 1981), is still young. No comparisons will be drawn here between our analytical methods and style with others in this area, but instead some comments about the overall approach used in this volume will be provided, concerning when and how it can be applied in other fields.

The basis for any taxonomy, whether empirical or not, is a working definition of the unit of analysis. Forgas (1980) provides an excellent review of the problems involved in defining the concept of a social episode. It is not uncommon for major fields of inquiry to contain widespread confusion regarding the most basic concepts. Such problems have beset those who study situations (cf. Argyle, 1979), social structure (cf. Manicas, 1980), and culture (cf. the classic discussion of competing definitions in Kroeber and Kluckhohn, 1952). Sufficient agreement must exist in a field concerning the unit of analysis and its definition before a taxonomic overview can be attempted.

An empirically based taxonomy which uses human judgements involves several additional problems regarding the definition of what is to be analysed. First, the concept used for the unit of analysis must make sense to the people whose judgements form the basis for the taxonomy. It is not sufficient for a theorist to derive a sophisticated conceptual definition if respondents are unable to share that definition. Hence, any empirical approach to taxonomic meta-analysis is constrained by common-sense language and definitions, although it is worth mentioning here that these constraints are no greater than those which apply to many paper-and-pencil attitude tests of questionnaires.

The researcher need not be as constrained by ordinary definitions, however, if he elects to use experts as judges. The decision of whom to use as judges is crucial in taxonomy construction. In virtually all the human sciences, there is a tension between the tendency for researchers to impose their definitions on respondents' thoughts and actions, and the desire to study people on their own terms. Cultural anthropologists adopted linguistic terminology to distinguish between these two options: the "emic" and "etic" perspectives (see Pelto, 1970, for a discussion of these concepts and the anthropological debates sparked off by them). An etic taxonomy is one based on researcher or expert judgements regarding the similarities or differences among the units of analysis, as exemplified by Wispé's taxonomy of helping terms. The taxonomy developed in this volume is emic, insofar as it is based on subjects' perceptions of helping.

Which approach one takes depends, of course, on whose judgements are important or relevant. In our case, the decision to adopt an emic approach was based on an initial stance that people's definitions of situations are important influences on their responses to those situations. In order areas of inquiry it might make more sense to use social psychologists as judges, a case for which is briefly made in the next section. Although this distinction may be obvious, social psychologists in the field of helping research neglected it when they overemphasized certain kinds of helping and excluded others which play an important role in everyday social life.

Finally, there is the issue of the domain which the taxonomy should cover. Without a clear definition of the limits to the field, no taxonomy can be assessed for its definitiveness. The results from the Chapter 3 study are an illustration of one method for specifying a domain, which of course was emic and used a natural language lexicon of helping terms. An etic approach to domain specification might not use natural language categories at the outset, but it would require some kind of lexical list, containing at least some generic terms which judges could use for determining when an item is inside or outside of the field. We would advise researchers to use as detailed a lexicon as is feasible, since some evidence in studies of ordinary language categorization suggests that generic categories do not always satisfactorily cover the referent domain (Kempton, 1978).

Implications for Social Psychology

The present volume, it has already been argued, has implications for the topic of helping, for research methodology in social psychology and, to a lesser extent, for individuals and organizations involved in the helping process. In addition there is a more general level of implication which warrants attention. In the first chapter four major criticisms of social psychology as a whole were outlined. These criticisms can be listed as follows: (1) the lack of cumulative research, (2) laboratory experiments which lack ecological validity, (3) an overly deterministic view of human action, and (4) a failure to provide insightful social criticism and alternatives. If the present research has managed to address some of these general criticisms, then it follows that there may well be implications for researchers studying other topics in social psychology. It is the opinion of the authors that the present volume has achieved some success in relation to criticism (1) in the above list and that the general style of research discussed has unearthed some tangential points which bear on the second, third and fourth criticisms. The general implications of the present volume for other areas of inquiry will be discussed by reconsidering these four critical perspectives.

The Issue of Non-cumulative Research

The view that non-cumulative research is a central concern in social psychology is intimately linked to the role of theory and theory construction in the discipline (cf. McGuire, 1980). It has been argued both in this chapter and in Chapters 3 and 6 in particular that a taxonomy of helping facilitates the integration of research findings by providing a framework through which studies can be compared and evaluated. Using the taxonomy researchers can reconcile apparent contradictions in the literature (such as the study of sex differences in helping discussed in this chapter), and plan their studies more precisely. Perhaps more importantly the range of convenience or generality of each theoretical perspective can be more carefully delineated by relating the relevance of an approach, such as attribution theory, to a certain segment of the taxonomy.

This kind of organized use of a taxonomy or pre-theoretical framework to compare and guide research studies and theories may be contrasted with the typical research-overview approach adopted in integrative journal articles. In publications such as *Psychological Bulletin,* authors frequently attempt to synthesize contradictory research findings which are from methodologically different studies. The approach of the skilful writers to such a daunting task may be portrayed as follows. The literature is reviewed by using two search principles, one of frequency counting, and secondly, one of methodological triangulation. That is, emphasis is given to research findings which occur frequently but which also hold up when different methodological approaches are employed. Contradictory findings are explained on the basis of a creative list of possibilities which include research method and design, the choice of subjects, measurement problems; or through elaborating the theoretical perspective to include a subset of cases which are accounted for by the operation of additional variables.

It can be argued that this model of the conventional review process contains, at least in the researchers' mind, an implicit taxonomy of that particular area of inquiry. The explanations reviewers give to differentiate areas of the implicit taxonomic space are analogous to the dimensions which define the helping taxonomy discussed in this volume. Perceptive reviewers choose dimensions which are supported by subsequent research findings.

A comparison between this review process and the kind of research organization attempted in this volume raises four issues. First, it is apparent that the conventional method of writing a research review or a literature introduction involves many implicit organizational processes for the researcher. A more explicit discussion of these processes and the advantage of using a specific taxonomic multidimensional procedure as a model for this process warrants further inquiry. The second and third implications refer to two similar procedures for deriving a taxonomy of an area. Consider, for example, the topic of conformity. It can be argued that the plethora of studies concerned with conformity would also be suitable for the kind of *post-hoc* taxonomic organization using the participant's perspective which has been adopted for the helping literature. Subjects would be asked to compare the similarities of such situations as the Sherif experiment and the Asch study in order to provide an organizational overview of the properties or character of studies done in the conformity area. Some projected regions of a conformity space might well include studies of laboratory conformity where one person is influenced by many, conformity studies where the majority is influenced by the minority (cf.

Moscovici), and more public instances of conformity such as those involving fads and fashions.

For some areas of inquiry it might be argued that research participants cannot readily understand the distinctions among the studies. For example, researchers may want to derive a taxonomy for the conformity studies which has as its framework only the laboratory studies of conformity. In this instance the task might be to discriminate among various modified versions of the Asch, Sherif and Krutchfield procedures. For such a task a subject pool of social psychologists might well be the most appropriate group to act as research participants. This approach would have the particular advantage, as compared to the conventional procedures of reviewing an area, of combining the insights and understanding of a group of highly skilled informants.

An even more desirable approach to the problem of non-cumulative research lies in establishing a taxonomy before the field of inquiry is replete with unrelated studies. Perhaps one such topic area which is still a candidate for this approach is that of love. For a complex of reasons, including research funding, scientific respectability and methodological inadequacy, love relationships have been relatively lightly researched in social psychology (Rubin, 1973; Walster and Walster, 1978). As Huston and Levinger (1978:116) argue, "there exists no comprehensive classification of relationships, a problem which is beginning to be recognised". This comment resembles, of course, many of the pleas for a taxonomy of helping which were outlined in Chapter 1. Forgas and Dobosz (1979) have attempted to provide a classification scheme of relationships in a student milieu and more work of this kind applied to a larger context would be most timely. It can be suggested that if such a classification is produced it will considerably enhance the development of the social psychology of love by providing a framework to guide and compare future studies.

In summary, several suggestions for social psychologists emerge from the criticism that the area is not cumulative. These include establishing a taxonomy before the topic is thoroughly researched, deriving a taxonomy from the perspective of participants and using other social psychologists to discriminate among complex and hard-to-communicate studies. It is also suggested that the process of reviewing areas of inquiry should itself be examined and the possibility for reviewers to use an implicit multidimensional taxonomy as an analogy of the review process was suggested.

The Issue of Ecological Validity

The principal implication of the taxonomic approach for the issue of ecological validity is to provide an overview of the focus and concentration of studies in an area. Thus, a sense of balance or imbalance between laboratory studies and observation of natural behaviours may be established. For helping, it was established in Chapter 3 that personal intimate forms of helping were severely under-represented in the helping literature. It is also to be hoped that a knowledge of the helping space as a whole will enable researchers working in the experimental tradition to think about the kinds of behaviours they are trying to simulate in the laboratory. An analogy may be drawn here from the field of crowd behaviour. Clearly there are many types of crowds: expressive crowds, baiting crowds, aggressive crowds and passive crowds. Researchers who attempt to understand the processes of shaping crowd behaviour typically design research situations which approximate only one of these crowd types. Even if the researchers themselves are aware of the problem, the findings from such studies are frequently applied to crowds in general (Mann, Innes and Newton, 1980). Such a generalization involves two kinds of errors. First, there is the ubiquitous problem of the faithfulness of the experiment findings to the non-laboratory context and, secondly, there is the issue of the kind of non-laboratory context to which the findings might apply. Again it can be argued that a taxonomy of studies might assist in this context by providing a dimensional interpretation of the relationship between the laboratory setting and the natural crowd settings. Thus, while it is anticipated that laboratory contexts will rarely be as extreme as real crowds along such dimensions as aggression, it would at least be useful to know which laboratory manipulations most resemble crowds of various types. Such an approach does not of course solve the issue of ecological validity, but at least it draws attention to the most appropriate natural setting to which the experimental study might apply.

The Issue of Determinism of Human Action

The most relevant account of a non-deterministic approach to helping provided in this volume was the material discussed in Chapter 6. The second and third studies discussed in that chapter were concerned with helping situations in which subjects were involved on a daily basis. These were the kinds of settings which participants chose for themselves and reacted to as they pleased. It was demonstrated that the dimensions of the category scheme which were used to characterize research studies of helping were also applicable to these everyday helping episodes. An interesting suggestion can also be made in relation to the pattern of helping findings and the issue of the control of behaviour. While a definitive search of the literature on this issue has not been made and is beyond the scope of this chapter, it appears that the search for individual variables influencing prosocial behaviour has often proved fruitless in experimental situations. On the other hand, in questionnaire and archival material, in interviews and in observational data, the individual's experiences and values appear to be more closely tied to instances of helping (cf. Staub, 1978). This suggests that with some forms of helping, notably those in naturally occurring situations, individual characteristics and the participant's cognition may be crucial in determining his or her behaviour. In the unfamiliar confines of the experimental setting, the broad tendency of most studies is to situationally control the subjects' responses and thereby prompt an appropriately deterministic account of behaviour. The implication of this generalization for social psychologists concerned with issues of determinism and the control of behaviour may well lie in redesigning experimental situations to permit a much greater range of responses and behaviours. If individual characteristics then correlate more closely with observed behaviours, it is possible that the appropriateness of deterministic and non-deterministic accounts for different kinds of social settings will be better understood.

The Issue of Innovatory Social Thinking

It can be argued that social psychology, in common with psychology generally as well as other social sciences, has a responsibility to provide material to stimulate public discussion and help shape social policy. However, naïve recommendations stemming from an overly simplistic account of behaviour are also likely to be damaging to the psychologist. Accordingly, research recommendations need to be sufficiently subtle to respect individual differences and retain reasonable predictive power. Little research effort has been directed towards these larger issues in this volume. However, it can be argued that an understanding of a field of behaviour through the organizational framework provided in this volume can assist the evaluation of social ideas, as was previously discussed in regard to the helping professions. Consider, for example, the notion that criminals and in particular juvenile offenders should be involved in forms of community reparation through planned helping episodes. Rarely is any thought given to the type of helping to be done and the appropriateness of this form of helping for the personality and goals of the offender. The effectiveness of community service programs for criminal offenders could be systematically understood by comparing effectiveness across different clusters of helping tasks for matched groups of offenders. Such analysis might locate types of helping which both benefit the community and suit the personality and retraining needs of the offender.

The constructs which different community groups use to describe the same cluster of social episodes could also form the basis for action-oriented attempts to solve conflict situations, as suggested in the Chapter 4 analysis of political party differences, While it is transparently clear that groups in conflict can mutually understand one another's perspective but still not come to terms with the conflict situation due to powerful ideological pressures, it is also unlikely that intervening parties can provide innovative social solutions without understanding the perspective of the rival factions. In this modest way an understanding of the episodes may assist social problem solving.

Finally, it is a truism that most topics in social psychology warrant further study. It is hoped, following the emphasis of this volume, that providing an organizing framework for fields of research in social psychology receives high priority as an appropriate topic for future efforts.

References

Adams, B. N. (1967) Interaction theory and the social network. *Sociometry*, **30**, 64–78.

Alker, H. A. (1972) Is personality situationally specific or intropsychically consistent? *Journal of Personality*, **40**, 1–16.

Allison, P. D. (1978) Measures of inequality. *American Sociological Review*, **43**, 865–880.

Amato, P. (1978) City versus country: Friendliness and helping behaviour in Queensland. Paper presented at the Sociological Association of Australia and New Zealand Conference, Brisbane, Australia.

Amato, P. R. (1981a) Urban–rural differences in helping: Behaviour in Australia and the United States. *Journal of Social Psychology*, 1981, *114*, 289–290.

Amato, P. R. (1981b) The effects of environmental complexity and pleasantness on prosocial behaviour: A field study. *Australian Journal of Psychology*, 33, 285–295.

Amato, P. R. (1981c) The impact of the built environment on prosocial behaviour: A field study of the Townsville City Mall. *Australian Journal of Psychology*, 33, 297–303.

Amato, P. R. (1982) Prosocial behaviour in urban and rural environments: Field studies based upon a taxonomic organization of helping episodes. Doctoral Dissertation, James Cook University of North Queensland.

Arbib, M. (1964) *Brains, machines, and mathematics*. New York: McGraw-Hill.

Argyle, M. (1979) Social behaviour as a function of situations. In G. Ginsburg (Ed.) *Emerging strategies in social psychological research*. New York: Wiley.

Armistead, N. (1974) *Reconstructing social psychology*. Harmondsworth, Middx: Penguin.

Aronfreed, J. (1968) *Conduct and conscience*. New York: Academic Press.

Aronfreed, J. (1970) The socialization of altruistic and sympathetic behaviour: Some theoretical and experimental analyses. In J. Macaulay and L. Berkowitz (Eds.) *Altruism and helping behaviour*. New York: Academic Press.

Ashton, N. L. and Severy, L. J. (1976) Arousal and cost in bystander intervention. *Personality and Social Psychology Bulletin*, **2**, 268–272.

Backman, C. (1979) Epilogue: A new paradigm? In G. Ginsburg (Ed.) *Emerging strategies in social psychological research*. New York: Wiley.

Bandura, A. (1971) *Social learning theory*. Englewood Cliffs, N. J.: Prentice-Hall.

Barker, R. G. (1968) *Ecological psychology: Concepts and methods for studying the environment of human behaviour*. Stanford, California: Stanford University Press.

Barnes, R. D., Ickes, W. J. and Kidd, R. F. (1979) Effects of the perceived intentionality, and stability of anothers' dependency on helping behaviour. *Personality and Social Psychology Bulletin*, **5**, 367–372.

Bar-tal, D. (1976) *Prosocial behaviour*. New York: John Wiley & Sons.

Baumann, D. J., Cialdini, R. B. and Kenrick, D. T. (1981) Altruism as hedonism: Helping and self-gratification as equivalent responses. *Journal of Personality and Social Psychology*, **40**, 1039–1046.

Bell, W. and Boat, D. (1957) Urban neighbourhoods and informal social relations. *American Journal of Sociology*, **62**, 395.

Bem, D. and Allen, A. (1974) On predicting some of the people most of the time: The search for cross-situational consistencies in behaviour. *Psychological Review*, **81**, 506–520.

Bennett, J. F. and Hays, W. L. (1960) Multidimensional unfolding: Determining the dimensionality of ranked preference data. *Psychometrika*, **25**, 27–43.

Benson, P. L., Dehority, J., Garmon, L., Hanson, E., Hochschwender, M., Lebold, C., Rohr, R. and Sullivan, J. (1980) Intrapersonal correlates of nonspontaneous helping behaviour. *Journal of Social Psychology*, *110*, 87–95.

Bergin, A. E. (1975) When shrinks hurt: Psychotherapy can be dangerous. *Psychology Today*, *19*, 96–104.

Bergin, A. E. and Garfield, S. L. (Eds.) (1971) *Handbook of Psychotherapy and Behaviour Change*. New York: Wiley.

Berkowitz, L. (1966) A laboratory investigation of social class and national differences in helping behaviour. *International Journal of Psychology*, **1**, 231–240.

Berkowitz, L. (1969) Reactance to improper dependency relationships. *Journal of Experimental Psychology*, **5**, 283–294.

Berkowitz, L. (1972) Social norms, feelings, and other factors affecting helping behaviour and altruism. In L. Berkowitz (Ed.) *Advances in experimental social psychology*, Vol. 6. New York: Academic Press.

Berkowitz L. and Daniels, L. R., (1963) Responsibility and dependency. *Journal of Abnormal and Social Psychology*, **66**, 429–436.

Berkowitz, L. and Daniels, L. R., (1964) Affecting the salience of the social responsibility norm. *Journal of Abnormal and Social Psychology*, **68**, 302–306.

Berkowitz, L. and Lutterman, K. G. (1968) The traditionally socially responsible personality. *The Public Opinion Quarterly*, **32**, 169–185.

Bezdek, J. C. (1974) Numerical taxonomy with fuzzy sets. *Journal of Mathematical Biology*, **1**, 57–71.

Bickman, L. (1971) The effects of another bystander's ability to help in bystander intervention in an emergency. *Journal of Experimental Social Psychology*, **7**, 367–379.

Bickman, L. and Henchy, T. (1972) *Beyond the laboratory: Field research in social psychology*. New York: McGraw-Hill.

Bickman, L., Teger, A., Gabriele, T., McLaughlin, C., Berger, M. and Sunaday, E. (1973) Dormitory density and helping behaviour. *Environment and Behaviour*, **5**, 465–490.

Blalock, H. M., Jr. (1979) *Social statistics*, Second Edition. New York: McGraw-Hill.

Bloom, M. (1975) *The paradox of helping*. New York: Wiley.

Blumer, R. (1969) *Symbolic interactionism*. Englewood Cliffs: Prentice Hall.

Borg, I. and Lingoes, J. C. (1980) A model and algorithm for multidimensional scaling with external constraints on the distances. *Psychometrika*, **45**, 25–38.

Bott, E. (1971) *Family and social networks*. London: Tavistock,

Bowers, K. S., (1973) Situationalism in psychology. *Psychological Review*, **80**, 307–336.

Brehm, J. W. (1966) *A theory of psychological reactance*. New York: Academic Press.

Brehmer, B. and Hammond, K. R. (1977) Cognitive factors in interpersonal conflict. In D. Druckman (Ed.) *Negotiations: Social-psychological perspectives*. Beverly Hills, CA: Sage Publications.

Briar, S. (1967) The current crisis in social casework. In *Social work practice*. New York: Columbia University Press.

Bronfenbrenner, U. (1961) Some familial antecedents of responsibility and leadership in adolescents. In L. Petrulo and B. L. Bass (eds.) *Leadership and interpersonal behaviour*. New York: Holt.

Bryan, J. H. (1972) Why children help: A review. *Journal of Social Issues*, **28**, 87–104.

Bryan, J. H. and Test, M. A. (1967) Models and helping: Naturalistic studies in aiding behaviour. *Journal of Personality and Social Psychology*, **6**, 400–407.

Bryan, J. H. and Walbek, N. H. (1970) Preaching and practicing generosity: Children's actions and reactions. *Child Development*, **41**, 329–353.

Campbell, D. T. (1978) On the genetics of altruism and the counterhedonic components in human culture. In L. Wispé (Ed.) *Altruism, sympathy and helping. Psychological and sociological principles*. New York: Academic press.

Carkhuff, R. R. (1969) *Helping and human relations*, Volume II. New York: Holt, Rinehart & Winston.

Carroll, J. D. (1972) Individual differences and multidimensional scaling. In R. N. Shepard, A. K. Romney and S. B. Nerlove (Eds.) *Multidimensional Scaling: Theory and applications in the behavioural sciences*; Vol I. New York: Seminar Press.

Carroll, J. D. and Chang, J. J. (1970) Analysis of individual differences in multidimensional scaling via an N-way generalization of "Ekhart-Young" decomposition, *Psychometrika*, **35**, 283–319.

Carroll, J. D. and Chang, J. J. (1977) *The MDS(X) series of multidimensional scaling programs: INDSCAL program*. Report No. 36, University of Edinburgh Program Library Unit.

Carroll, J. D. and Chang, J. J. (1977) *The MDS(X) series of multidimensional scaling programs: PREFMAP program.* Report No. 38, University of Edinburgh Program Library Unit.

Carroll, J. D., Pruzansky, S. and Kruskal, J. B. (1980) CANDELINC: A general approach to multidimensional analysis of many-way arrays with linear constraints on parameters. *Psychometrika*, **45**, 3–24.

Cialdini, R. B., Darby, B. L. and Vincent, J. E. (1973) Transgression and altruism: A case for hedonism. *Journal of Experimental Social Psychology*, **9**, 502–516.

Cialdini, R. B. and Kenrick, D. T. (1976) Altruism as hedonism: A social development perspective on the relationship of negative mood state and helping. *Journal of Personality and Social Psychology*, **34**, 907–914.

Clark, R. D. and Word, L. E. (1974) Where is the apathetic bystander? Situational characteristics of the emergency. *Journal of Personality and Social Psychology*, **29**, 279–288.

Cohen, R. (1978) Altruism: Human, cultural, or what? In L. Wispé (Ed.) *Altruism, sympathy and helping. Psychological and sociological principles.* New York: Academic Press.

Coke, J. S., Batson, C. D. and McDavis, K. (1978) Empathic mediation of helping : A two stage model. *Journal of Personality and Social Psychology*, **36**, 752–766.

Collett, P. (1979) Personal construct theory and the repertory grid. In G. Ginsburg (Ed.) *Emerging strategies in social psychological research.* New York: Wiley.

Coxon, A. P. M. and Jones, C. L. (1978) *The images of occupational prestige.* London: MacMillan.

Darley, J. and Batson, C. (1973) "From Jerusalem to Jericho": A study of situational and dispositional variables in helping behaviour. *Journal of Personality and Social Psychology*, **27**, 100–108.

Darley, J. M., and Latané, B. (1968) Bystander intervention in emergencies: Diffusion of responsibility. *Journal of Personality and Social Psychology*, **10**, 202–214.

De Luca, A. and Termini, S. (1972) A definition of nonprobabilistic entropy in the setting of fuzzy-sets theory. *Information and control*, **20**, 301–312.

DePalma, D. J. (1974) Effects of social class, moral orientation, and severity of punishment on boys' moral responses to transgressions and generosity. *Developmental Psychology*, *10*, 890–900.

Derlega, V. J., Wilson, M. and Chaikin, A. L. (1976) Friendship and disclosure reciprocity. *Journal of Personality and Social Psychology*, **34**, 578–582.

Egan, G. (1975) *The skilled helper.* Monterey, CA: Brooke-Cole.

Ekehammer, B. (1974) Interactionism in psychology from a historical perspective. *Psychological Bulletin*, *81*, 1026–1048.

Eisenberg-Berg, N. and Neal, C. (1981) Children's moral reasoning about self and others: Effects of the story character and cost of helping. *Personality and Social Psychology Bulletin*, **7**, 17–23.

Ehlert, J., Ehlert, N and Merrens, M. (1973) The influence of ideological affiliation on helping behaviour. *Journal of Social Psychology*, **89**, 315–316.

Elliot, R. and Vasta, R. (1970) The modelling of sharing: Effect associated with vicarious reinforcement, symbolization, age, and generalization. *Journal of Experimental Child Psychology*, **10**, 8–15.

Emler, N. P. and Rushton, J. P. (1974) Cognitive-developmental factors in children's generosity. *British Journal of Social and Clinical Psychology*, **13**, 277–281.

Endler, N. S. and Magnusson, D. (1976) *Interactional psychology and personality.* Washington, D.C.: Hemisphere.

Falbo, T. (1977) Multidimensional scaling of power strategies. *Journal of Personality and Social Psychology*, **35**, 537–547.

Festinger, L. (1954) A theory of social comparison processes. *Human Relations*, **7**, 117–140.

Fischer, W. F. (1963) Sharing in pre-school children as a function of amount and type of reinforcement. *Genetic Psychology Monographs*, **68**, 215–245.

Forbes, G. and Gromoll, H. (1971) The lost-letter technique as a measure of social variables: Some exploratory findings. *Social Forces*, **50**, 113–115.

Forgas, J. P. (1976) The perception of social episodes: Categorical and dimensional representations of two different social mileus. *Journal of Personality and Social*

Psychology, **34**, 199–209.

Forgas, J. P. (1980) *Social episodes*. London: Academic Press.

Forgas, J. P. and Dobosz, B. (1979) Toward a taxonomy of heterosexual relationships: A multidimensional scaling approach. Paper presented at the Annual General Meeting of Australian Social Psychologists. Sydney.

Franck, K. A. (1980) Friends and strangers: The social experience of living in urban and non-urban settings. *Journal of Social Issues*, **36**, 52–69.

Frederiksen, N. (1972) Toward a taxonomy of situations. *American Psychologist*, **27**, 114–124.

Freedman, J. L., Wallington, S. A. and Bless, E. (1967) Compliance without pressure: The effects of guilt. *Journal of Personality and Social Psychology*, **7**, 117–124.

Fromm, E. (1957) *The art of loving*. London: Allen & Unwin.

Furnham, A. (1981) Personality and activity preference. *The British Journal of Social Psychology*, **20**, 57–68.

Gaertner, S. L. (1973) Helping behaviour and racial discrimination among liberals and conservatives. *Journal of Personality and Social Psychology*, **25**, 335–341.

Gaertner, S. L. and Bickman, L. (1971) Effects of race on the elicitation of helping behaviour: the wrong number technique. *Journal of Personality and Social Psychology*, **20**, 218–222.

Garfinkel, H. (1967) *Studies in Ethnomethodology*. Englewood Cliffs, New Jersey: Prentice Hall.

Garfinkel, H. (1973) The origins of the term "ethnomethodology". In R. Turner (Ed.) *Ethnomethodology*. Harmondsworth, Middlesex: Penguin.

Gelfand, D. M., Hartmann, D. P., Walker, P. and Page, B. (1973) Who reports shoplifters? A field-experimental study. *Journal of Personality and Social Psychology*, **25**, 276–285.

Gergen, K. J. (1978) Toward generative theory. *Journal of Personality and Social Psychology*, **36**, 11, 1344–1360.

Gergen, K., Ellsworth, P., Maslach, C and Seipel, M. (1975) Obligation, donor resources, and reactions to aid in 3 cultures. *Journal of Personality and Social Psychology*, **31**, 390–400.

Gergen, K. J., Gergen, M. M. and Meter, K. (1972) Individual orientations to prosocial behaviour. *Journal of Social Issues*, **28**, 105–130.

Gilmour, R. and Duck, S. (Eds.) (1980) *The development of social psychology*. London: Academic Press.

Ginsburg, G. P. (Ed.) (1979) *Emerging strategies in social psychological research*. London: Wiley.

Glass, G. V., McGraw B. and Smith, M. L. (1981) *Meta-analysis in social research*. Beverley Hills, CA: Sage Publications.

Goodstadt, M. S. (1971) Helping and refusal to help: A test of balance and reactance theories. *Journal of Experimental Social Psychology*, **7**, 610–622.

Gottlieb, B. J. (1978) The development and application of a classification scheme of informal helping behaviours. *Canadian Journal of Behavioural Science*, **10**, 105–115.

Gouldner, A. W. (1960) The norm of reciprocity: A preliminary statement. *American Sociological Review*, **25**, 161–179.

Graycar, A. (1979) *Welfare politics in Australia: A study in policy analysis*. Melbourne: MacMillan.

Green, F. P. and Schneider, F. W. (1974) Age differences in the behaviour of boys on three measures of altruism. *Child Development*, **45**, 248–251.

Gross, A. E. and Latané, J. G. (1974) Receiving help, reciprocation, and interpersonal attraction. *Journal of Applied Social Psychology*, **4**, 210–223.

Grusec, J. E. (1971) Power and the internalization of self-denial. *Child Development*, **42**, 93–105.

Hamilton, W. D. (1972) Altruism and related phenomena, mainly in social insects. *Annual Review of Ecology and Systematics*, **3**, 193–232.

Hansson, R. O. and Slade, K. M. (1977) Altruism toward a deviant in city and small town. *Journal of Applied Social Psychology*, **7**, 272–279.

Hansson, R. O., Slade, K. M. and Slade. P. S. (1978) Urban–rural responsiveness to an altruistic model. *Journal of Social Psychology*, **105**, 99–105.

Harré, R. and Secord, P. F. (1972) *The explanation of social behaviour*. Oxford: Basil Blackwell.

Harris, M. B. and Baudin, H. (1973) The language of altruism: The effects of language, dress, and ethnic group. *Journal of Social Psychology*, **91**, 37–41.

Harris, M. B. and Bays, G. (1973) Altruism and sex roles. *Psychological Reports*, **32**, 1002.

Harris, M. B. and Meyer, F. W. (1973) Dependency, threat, and helping. *Journal of Social Psychology*, **90**, 239–242.

Harris, S., Mussen, P. and Rutherford, E. (1976) Some cognitive, behavioural and personality correlates of maturity of moral judgement. *Journal of Genetic Psychology*, **128**, 123–135.

Hartigan, J. A. (1975) *Clustering algorithms*, New York: Wiley.

Hartshorne, H., May, M. A. and Maller, J. B. (1929) *Studies in the nature of character;* Vol. II: *Studies in service and self-control*. New York: MacMillan.

Hatfield, E., Walster, G. W. and Piliavin, J. A. (1978) Equity theory and helping relationships. In L. Wispé (Ed.) *Altruism, sympathy and helping. Psychological and sociological principles*. New York: Academic Press.

Heider, F. (1958) *The psychology of interpersonal relations*. New York: Wiley.

Hersch, H. M. and Caramazza, A. (1976) A fuzzy-set approach to modifiers and vagueness in natural language. *Journal of Experimental Psychology*, **105**, 254–276.

Hoffman, M. L. (1976) Empathy, role-taking, guilt, and the development of altruistic motives. In T. Likona (Ed.) *Moral development and behaviour*. New York: Holt.

Hoffman, M. L. (1977) Sex differences in empathy and related behaviours. *Psychological Bulletin*, **84**, 712–720.

Hornstein, H. A. (1972) Promotive tension: The basis of prosocial behaviour from a Lewinian perspective. *Journal of Social Issues*, **28**, 191–218.

Hornstein, H. A. (1978) Promotive tension and prosocial behaviour: A Lewinian analysis. In L. Wispé, *Altruism, sympathy and helping*. New York: Academic Press.

House, J. S. and Wolf, S. (1978) Effects of urban residence on interpersonal trust and helping behaviour. *Journal of Personality and Social Psychology*, **36**, 1029–1043.

Huston, T. L. and Levinger, G. (1978) Interpersonal attraction and relationships. *Annual Review of Psychology*, **29**, 115–156.

Huston, T. L., Ruggiero, M., Conner, R. and Geis, G. (1981) Bystander intervention into crime: A study based upon naturally-occurring episodes. *Social Psychology Quarterly*, **44**, 14–23.

Ickes, W. J. and Kidd, R. F. (1976) An attributional analysis of helping behaviour. In J. H. Harvey, W. J. Ickes and R. F. Kidd (Eds.) *New directions in attribution research* (Vol. 1). Hillsdale, N.J.: Erlbaum.

Ickes, E. J., Kidd, R. F. and Berkowitz, L. (1976) Attributional determinants of monetary help-giving. *Journal of Personality*, **44**, 163–178.

Innes, J. M. (1980) Fashions in social psychology. In R. Gilmour and S. Duck (Eds.) *The development of social psychology*. London: Academic Press.

Isen, A. M. and Levin, P. F. (1972) Effect of feeling good on helping: Cookies and kindness. *Journal of Personality and Social Psychology*, **21**, 384–388.

Johnson, S. C. (1967) Hierarchical clustering schemes. *Psychometrika*, **32**, 241–254.

Kasarda, J. D. and Janowitz, M. (1974) Community attachment in mass society. *American Sociological Review*, **39**, 328–339.

Kaufmann, A. (1975) *Theory of fuzzy sets*, Vol. 1. New York: Academic Press.

Kay, P. and McDaniel, C. K. (1975) Colour categories as fuzzy sets. Working Paper No. 4. Berkeley: Language Behaviour Research Laboratory, University of California.

Kelley, H. H. (1967) Attribution theory in social psychology. In D. Levine (Ed.) *Nebraska Symposium on Motivation* (Vol. 15). Lincoln: University of Nebraska Press.

Kelley, K., and Byrne, D. (1976) Attraction and altruism: With a little help from my friends. *Journal of Research in Personality*, **10**, 59–68.

Kempton, W. (1978) Category grading and taxonomic relations: A mug is a sort of cup. *American Ethnologist*, **5**, 44–65.

Key, W. H. (1968) Rural–urban social participation. In S. F. Fava (Ed.) *Urbanism in world perspective*. New York: Crowell.

Knopfmacher, K. (1975) On measures of fuzziness. *Journal of Mathematical Analysis and Applications*, **49**. 529–534.

Kochen, M. (1975) Applications of fuzzy-set theory to psychology. In L. A. Zadeh (Ed.) *Fuzzy sets and their application to cognitive and decision processes*. New York: Academic Press.

Kochen, M. and Badre, A. N. (1974) On the precision of adjectives which denote fuzzy sets. *Journal of Cybernetics*, **4**, 49–59.

Kohlberg, L. (1969) Stage and sequence: The cognitive-development approach to socialization. In D. Goslin (Ed.) *Handbook of socialization theory and research*. Chicago: Rand McNally.

Kohlberg. L. (1976) Moral stages and moralization: The cognitive-developmental approach. In T. Likona (Ed.) *Moral development and behaviour*. New York: Holt.

Korte, C. and Ayvalioglu, N. (1981) N. Helpfulness in Turkey: Cities, towns and urban villages. *Journal of Cross-cultural Psychology* (in press).

Korte, C. and Kerr, N. (1975) Response to altruistic opportunities in urban and non-urban settings. *Journal of Social Psychology*, **95**, 183–184.

Korte, C., Ypma, I. and Toppen, A. (1975) Helpfulness in Dutch society as a function of urbanization and environment input level. *Journal of Personality and Social Psychology*, **32**, 996–1003.

Kraut, R. E. (1973) Effects of social labeling on giving to charity. *Journal of Experimental Social Psychology*, **9**, 551–562.

Krebs, D. L. (1975) Empathy and altruism. *Journal of Personality and Social Psychology*, **32**, 1134–1146.

Krebs, D. (1978) A cognitive-development approach to altruism. In L. Wispé (Ed.) *Altruism, sympathy, and helping. Psychological and sociological principles*. New York: Academic Press.

Kroeber, A. L. and Kluckhohn, C. (1952) Culture: A critical review of concepts and definitions. *Papers of the Peabody Museum of American Archaeology and Ethnology*, Harvard University, Cambridge, Mass.

Krupat, E. and Coury, M. (1975) The lost-letter technique and helping: An urban–non-urban comparison. Paper presented at a meeting of the American Psychological Association, Chicago.

Kruskal, J. B. and Wish, M. (1978) Multidimensional scaling. *Sage University Paper Series on Quantitative Applications in the Social Sciences*, 07–11. Beverly Hills: Sage Publications.

Lakoff, G. (1973) Hedges: A study in meaning criteria and the logic of fuzzy concepts. *Journal of Philosophic Logic*, **2**, 458–507.

Langer, E. J. and Abelson, R. P. (1972) How to succeed in getting help without really dying: The semantics of asking a favour. *Journal of Personality and Social Psychology*, **8**, 26–32.

Latané, B. and Dabbs, J. M. (1975) Sex, group size, and helping in three cities. *Sociometry*, **38**, 180–194.

Latané, B. and Darley, J. M. (1968) Group inhibition of bystander intervention. *Journal of Personality and Social Psychology*, **10**, 215–221.

Latané, B. and Darley, J. M. (1970) *The unresponsive bystander: Why doesn't he help?* New York: Appleton-Crofts.

Lau, S. and Blake, B. F. (1976) *Recent research on helping behaviour: An overview and bibliography* (ms. 1289). Washington, D.C.: Journal Supplement Abstract Service of the American Psychological Association.

Lay, C., Allen M. and Kassirer, A. (1974) The responsive bystander in emergencies: Some preliminary data. *The Canadian Psychologist*, **15**, 220–227.

Lerner, M. J. (1974) Social psychology of justice and interpersonal attraction. In T. Huston (Ed.) *Foundations of interpersonal attraction*. New York: Academic Press.

Lerner, M. J. (Ed.) (1975) The justice motive in social behaviour. *Journal of Social Issues*, **31**, 1–20.

Lerner, M. J. and Reavy, P. (1975) Locus of control, perceived responsibility for prior fate, and helping behaviour. *Journal of Research in Personality*, **9**, 1–20

Levine, C. (1976) Role-taking standpoint and adolescent usage of Kohlberg's conventional stages of moral reasoning. *Journal of Personality and Social Psychology*, **34**, 41–47.

Levine, M. E., Vilena, J., Altman, D. and Nadien, M. (1976) Trust of the stranger: An urban/small town comparison. *The Journal of Psychology*, **92**, 113–116.

Liebhart, E. H. (1972) Empathy and emergency helping: The effect of personality, self-concern, and acquaintance. *Journal of Experimental Social Psychology*, **8**, 404–411.

Litwak, E. and Szelenyi, I. (1969) Primary group structures and their functions: Kin, neighbours and friends. *American Sociological Review*, **34**, 465–481.

London, P. (1970) The rescuers: Motivational hypotheses about Christians who saved Jews from the Nazis. In J. Macaulay and L. Berkowitz (Eds.) *Altruism and helping behaviour*. New York: Academic Press.

Loo, S. G. (1977) Measures of fuzziness. *Cybernetica*, **20**, 201–207.

McGuire, W. J. (1980) The development of theory in social psychology. In R. Gilmour and S. Duck (Eds.) *The development of social psychology*. London: Academic Press.

MacVicar-Whelan, P. J. (1974) Fuzzy sets, the concept of height and the hedge "very". *Technical Memorandum 1*, Physics Dept. Grand Valley State College, Allendale, Michigan.

Manicas, P. (1980) The concept of social structure. *Journal for the Theory of Social Behaviour*, **10**, 65–82.

Mann, L., Innes, J. M. and Newton, J. (1980) Effects of anonymity/identifiability and group norm on aggression. Paper presented at 9th annual meeting of Australian Social Psychologists, Melbourne.

Mathews, K. E., Jr. and Canon, L. K. (1975) Environmental noise level as a determinant of helping behaviour. *Journal of Personality and Social Psychology*, **32**, 571–577.

Mehrabian, A. and Epstein, N. (1972) A measure of emotional empathy. *Journal of Personality*, **40**, 525–543.

Mehrabian, A. and Russell, J. A. (1974) *An approach to environmental psychology*. Cambridge, Massachusetts: M.I.T. Press.

Merrens, M. R. (1973) Nonemergency helping behaviour in various sized communities. *Journal of Social Psychology*, **90**, 327–328.

Meyer, J. P. and Mulherin, A. (1980) From attribution to helping: An analysis of the mediating effects of affect and expectancy. *Journal of Personality and Social Psychology*, **39**, 201–210.

Midlarsky, E., Bryan, J. H. and Brickman, P. (1973) Aversive approval: Interactive effects of modelling and reinforcement on altruistic behavior. *Child Development*, **44**, 321–328.

Milgram, S. (1963) Behavioural study of obedience. *Journal of Abnormal and Social Psychology*, **67**, 371–378.

Mims, P. R., Hartnett, J. J. and Nay, W. R. (1975) Interpersonal attraction and help volunteering as a function of physical attractiveness. *Journal of Psychology*, **89**, 125–131.

Mischel, W. (1968) *Personality and assessment*. New York: Wiley.

Mischel, W. (1976) *Introduction to Personality* (second ed.). New York: Holt.

Mixon, D. (1974) If you don't deceive, what can you do? In N. Armistead (Ed.) *Reconstructing social psychology*. Harmondsworth, Middlesex: Penguin.

Morgan, E. G. (1973) Situational specificity in altruistic behaviour. *Representative Research in Social Psychology*, **4**, 56–66.

Moscovici, S. (1976) *Social influence and social change*. London: Academic Press.

Nadler, A., Romek, E. and Shapiro-Friedman, A. (1979) Giving in the Kibbutz. *Journal of Cross-cultural Psychology*, **10**, 57–72.

Nisbett, R. and Wilson, T. (1977) Telling more than we can know: Verbal reports on mental processes. *Psychological Review*, **84**, 231–259.

O'Bryant, S.L. and Brophy, J. E. (1976) Sex differences in altruistic behaviour. *Development Psychology*, **12**, 554–555.

Page, R. A. (1977) Noise and helping behaviour. *Environment and Behaviour*, **84**, 231–259.

Pearce, P. (1980) Strangers, travellers, and Greyhound terminals: a study of small scale helping behaviours. *Journal of Personality and Social Psychology*, **38**, 935–940.

Pelto, P. J. (1970) *Anthropological research: The structure of inquiry*. New York: Harper & Row.

Piaget, J. (1932) *The moral judgement of the child*. London: Kegan Paul, Trench, & Trubner.

Piliavin, I. M., Rodin, J. and Piliavin, J. A. (1969) Good Samaritanism: An underground phenomena? *Journal of Personality and Social Psychology*, **13**, 289–299.

Piliavin, J. A. and Piliavin, I. M. (1972) Effect of blood on reactions to a victim. *Journal of Personality and Social Psychology*, **23**, 353–362.

Pomazal, R. J. and Clore, G. L. (1973) Helping on the highway: The effects of dependency and sex. *Journal of Applied Social Psychology*, **3**, 150–164.

Pomazal, R. J. and Jaccard, J. J. (1976) An informational approach to altruistic behaviour. *Journal of Personality and Social Psychology*, **33**, 317–327.

Raymond, B. J. and Unger, R. K. (1972) "The apparel oft proclaims the man." Co-operation with deviant and conventional youth. *Journal of Social Psychology*, **87**, 75–82.

Reiss, A. J. (1959) Rural-urban and status differences in interpersonal contacts. *American Journal of Sociology*, **65**, 182–195.

Rosch, E. H. (1973) On the internal structure of perceptual and semantic categories. In T. M. Moore (Ed.) *Cognitive development and the acquisition of language*. New York: Academic Press.

Rosenbaum, R. M. A. (1972) A dimensional analysis of the perceived causes of success and failure (Doctoral Dissertation, University of California, Los Angeles). *Dissertation Abstracts International*, **33**, 5040B.

Rosenhan, D. (1970) The natural socialization of altruistic autonomy. In J. Macaulay and L. Berkowitz (Eds.) *Altruism and helping behaviour*. New York: Academic Press.

Rosenhan, D. L. (1978) Toward resolving the altruism paradox: Affect, self-reinforcement, cognition. In L. Wispé (Ed.) *Altruism, sympathy, helping. Psychological and sociological principles*. New York: Academic Press.

Rosenhan, D. and White, G. (1967) Observation and rehearsal as determinants of prosocial behaviour. *Journal of Personality and Social Psychology*, **5**, 424–431.

Rosenhan, D. L., Underwood, B. and Moore, B. (1974) Affect moderates self-gratification and altruism. *Journal of Personality and Social Psychology*, **30**, 546–552.

Rosenthal, A. M. (1964) *Thirty-eight Witnesses*. New York: McGraw-Hill.

Roskam, E. E., and Lingoes, J. C. (1977) *The MDS(X) series of multidimensional scaling programs: MINISSA program*. Report No. 32.

Rotton, J. (1977) Sex, residential location, and altruism. *Psychological Reports*, **40**, 102.

Rubin, K. H. and Schneider, F. W. (1973) The relationship between moral judgement, ego-centrism, and altruistic behaviour. *Child Development*, **44**, 661–665.

Rubin, Z. (1973) *Liking and loving: An introduction to social psychology*. New York: Holt.

Rudestam, K. E., Richards, D. L. and Garrison, P. (1971) Effect of self-esteem on an unobtrusive measure of altruism. *Psychological Reports*, **29**, 847–851.

Rushton, J. P. (1973) Generosity in children: Immediate and long-term effects of modeling, preaching and moral judgement. *Journal of Personality and Social Psychology*, **31**, 459–466.

Rushton, J. P. (1978) Urban density and altruism: Helping strangers in a Canadian city, suburb, and small town. *Psychological Reports*, **43**, 987–990.

Rushton, J. P. (1980) *Altruism, socialization & society*. Englewood Cliffs, New Jersey: Prentice-Hall.

Ruspini, E. (1969) A new approach to clustering. *Information and Control*, **15**, 22–32.

Sampson, E. E. (1978) Scientific paradigms and social values: Wanted a scientific revolution. *Journal of Personality and Social Psychology*, **36**, 11, 1332–1343.

Schneider, F. W., Lesko, W. A. and Garrett, W. A. (1980) Helping behaviour in hot, comfortable, and cold temperatures: A field-study. *Environment and Behaviour*, **12**, 231–240.

Schneider, F. W. and Mockus, Z. (1975) Failure to find a rural–urban difference in incidence of altruistic behaviour. *Psychological Reports*, **35**, 294.

Schopler, J. and Bateson, N. (1965) The power of dependence. *Journal of Personality and Social Psychology*, **2**, 247–254.

Schopler, J. and Thompson, V. (1968) Role of attribution processes in mediating amount of reciprocity for a favour. *Journal of Personality and Social Psychology*, **10**, 243–250.

Schreiber, S. T. and Glidewell, J. C. (1978) Social norms and helping in a community of limited liability. *American Journal of Community Psychology*, **6**, 441–453.

Schwartz, S. H. (1970) Elicitation of moral obligation and self-sacrificing behaviour: An experimental study of volunteering to be a bone marrow donor. *Journal of Personality and Social Psychology*, **15**, 283–293.

Schwartz, S. H. (1973) Normative explanations of helping behaviour: A critique, proposal, and empirical test. *Journal of Experimental Social Psychology*, **9**, 349–364.

Schwartz, S. H. (1974) Awareness of interpersonal consequences, responsibility denial, and volunteering. *Journal of Personality and Social Psychology*, **30**, 57–63.

Schwartz, S. H. (1977) Normative influences on altruism. In L. Berkowitz (Ed.) *Advances in experimental social psychology*, Vol. 10. New York: Academic Press.

Schwartz, S. H. and Ben David, A. (1976) Responsibility and helping in an emergency: Effects of blame, ability and denial of responsibility. *Sociometry*, **39**, 406–415.

Schwartz, S. H. and Clausen, G. T. (1970) Responsibility, norms, and helping in an emergency. *Journal of Personality and Social Psychology*, **16**, 299–310.

Schutz, A. (1970) *On phenomenology and social relations*. Chicago: University of Chicago Press.

Sherrod, D. R. and Downs, R. (1974) Environmental determinants of altruism: The effects of stimulus overload and perceived control on helping. *Journal of Experimental Social Psychology*, **10**, 468–479.

Shotland, R. L. and Huston, T. K. (1979) Emergencies: What are they and do they influence bystanders to intervene? *Journal of Personality and Social Psychology*, **37**, 1822–1834.

Smale, G. G. (1977) *Prophecy, behaviour and change*. London: Routledge & Kegan Paul.

Smith, R., Vanderbilt, K and Callen, M. (1973) Social comparison and bystander intervention in emergencies. *Journal of Applied Social Psychology*, **3**, 186–196.

Smithson, M. (1979) The Tangepera-Ray generalized index of concentration: further generalizations. *Sociological Methods and Research*, **8**, 123–142.

Smithson, M. (1981) Measurement and probability models for fuzzy nominal data. *Theory and Decision*, **13** (in press).

Smithson, M. (1982) Applications of fuzzy-set concepts to behavioural sciences. *Journal of Mathematical Social Sciences* (accepted for publication).

Sokal, R. R., and Sneath, P. H. A. (1963) *Principles of numerical taxonomy*. London: W.H. Freeman.

Staub, E. (1974) Helping a distressed person: Social, personality, and stimulus determinates. In L. Berkowitz (Ed.) *Advances in experimental social psychology*, Vol. 7. New York: Academic Press.

Staub, E. (1978) *Positive social behaviour and morality* (Vol. 1). New York: Academic Press.

Staub, E. (1979) *Positive social behaviour and morality* (Vol. 2). New York: Academic Press.

Staub, E. and Baer, R. S., Jr. (1974) Stimulus characteristics of a sufferer and difficulty of escape as determinants of helping. *Journal of Personality and Social Psychology*, **30**, 279–284.

Strickland, L. J., Aboud, F. E. and Gergen, K. J. (Eds.) (1976) *Social psychology in transition*. New York: Plenum Press.

Sutcliffe, J. P. and Crabbe, B. D. (1963) Incidence and degrees of friendship in urban and rural areas. *Social Forces*, **42**, 60–67.

Taagepera, R. and Ray, J. L. (1977) A generalized index of concentration. *Sociological Methods of Research*, **5**, 367–384.

Takooshian, H., Haber, S. and Lucido, D. (1977) Who wouldn't help a lost child? You maybe. *Psychology Today*, **10**, 67.

Theil, H. (1967) *Economics and Information Theory*. Chicago: Rand-McNally.

Trimakas, K. A., and Nicolay, R. C. (1974) Self-concept and altruism in old age. *Journal of Gerontology*, **29**, 434–439.

Trivers, R. L. (1971) The evolution of reciprocal altruism. *Quarterly Review of Biology*, **46**, 35–57.

Truax, C. B. and Mitchell, K. M. (1971) Research on certain therapist interpersonal skills in relation to process and outcome. In Bergin, A. E., and Garfield, S. L. (*op.cit.*).

Tucker, L. R. and Messick, S. (1963) An individual difference model for multidimensional scaling. *Psychometrika*, **28**, 333–367.

Walster, E. and Walster, G. W. (1978) *A new look at love*. Reading, Mass: Addison-Wesley.

Walster, E., Walster, G. W. and Berscheid, E. (1978) *Equity: Theory and research*. Boston: Allyn & Bacon.

Weiner, B. (Ed.) (1974) *Achievement motivation and attribution theory*. Morristown, N.J.: General Learning Press.

Weiner, B. (1980) A cognitive (attribution)–emotion–action model of motivated behaviour: An analysis of judgements of help-giving. *Journal of Personality and Social Psychology*, **39**, 186–200.

Weiner, B., Russell, D. and Lerman, D. (1979) The cognitive-emotional process in achievement-related contexts. *Journal of Personality and Social Psychology*, **37**, 1211–1220.

Weiner, F. H. (1976) Altruism, ambiance, and action: The effects of rural and urban rearing on helping behaviour. *Journal of Personality and Social Psychology*, **34**, 112–124.

Weissbrod, C. S. (1976) Noncontingent warmth induction, cognitive style, and children's imitative donation and rescue effort behaviours. *Journal of Personality and Social Psychology*, **34**, 274–281.

West, S. G., Whitney, G. and Schnedler, R. (1975) Helping a motorist in distress. The effects of sex, race and neighbourhood. *Journal of Personality and Social Psychology*, **31**, 691–698.

Wexler, K. and Romney, A. K. (1972) Individual variations in cognitive structures. In A. K. Romney, R. N. Shepard, and S. B. Nerlove, (Eds.) *Multidimensional scaling: Theory and applications in the behavioural sciences*; Vol. II. New York: Seminar Press.

White, G. M. (1972) Immediate and deferred effects of model observation and guided and unguided rehearsal on donating and stealing. *Journal of Personality and Social Psychology*, **21**, 139–148.

Wilson, E. O. (1975) *Sociobiology: The new synthesis*. Cambridge, Massachusetts: The Belknap Press of Harvard University Press.

Wish, M., Deutsch, M. and Biener, L. (1972) Differences in perceived similarity of nations. In Romney, A. K., Shepard, R. N. and Nerlove, S. B. (Eds.) *op cit.*

Wispé, L. G. (1972) Positive forms of social behaviour: An overview. *Journal of Social Issues*, **28**, 1–20.

Wispé, L. G. (1978) Toward an integration. In L. G. Wispé, *Altruism, sympathy and helping*. New York: Academic Press.

Wispé L. G. and Freshley, H. B. (1971) Race, sex, and sympathetic helping behaviour: The broken bag caper. *Journal of Personality and Social Psychology*, **17**, 59–65.

Wrightsman, L. (1964) Measurement of philosophies of human nature. *Psychological Reports*, **14**, 743–751.

Wynne-Edwards, V. C. (1962) *Animal dispersion in relation to social behaviour*. Edinburgh: Oliver & Boyd.

Zadeh, L. A. (1965) Fuzzy sets. *Information and Control*, **8**, 338–353.

Zysno, P. (1979) One class of operators for the aggregation of fuzzy sets. Paper presented at EURO III, Amsterdam.

Appendix 1:

	Attending to	Collaborating with	Cooperating	Doting on	Educating	Exonerating	Intervening	Showing kindness	Lending something	Ministering to	Reinforcing	Reviving	Soothing
01													
02													
03													
04													
05													
06													
07													
08													
09													
10													
11													
12													
13													
14													
15													
16													
17													
18													
19													
20													
21													
22													
23													
24													
25													
26													
27													
28													
29													
30													

Appendix 2
Intercategory Overlap Matrix

Categories	01	02	03	04	05	06	07	08	09	10	11	12	13	14	15	16	17	18
01	—																	
02	.62	—																
03	.61	.34	—															
04	.77	.80	.59	—														
05	.66	.95	.37	.83	—													
06	.94	.72	.53	.83	.78	—												
07	.74	.75	.57	.89	.79	.83	—											
08	.86	.79	.61	.80	.85	.90	.80	—										
09	.90	.75	.48	.74	.78	.89	.74	.89	—									
10	.86	.67	.67	.83	.73	.83	.80	.89	.84	—								
11	.89	.81	.60	.81	.84	.88	.77	.93	.89	.85	—							
12	.73	.83	.45	.87	.89	.86	.79	.81	.73	.78	—							
13	.91	.75	.66	.84	.75	.86	.78	.89	.87	.92	.90	.77	—					
14	.85	.73	.64	.83	.80	.91	.82	.86	.78	.80	.83	.86	.81	—				
15	.71	.61	.67	.87	.67	.77	.87	.75	.62	.80	.66	.76	.76	.85	—			
16	.88	.81	.65	.88	.86	.91	.85	.94	.87	.92	.92	.85	.93	.89	.81	—		
17	.93	.74	.58	.85	.73	.91	.77	.83	.86	.85	.90	.79	.94	.85	.73	.90	—	
18	.66	.76	.34	.71	.82	.77	.79	.79	.76	.76	.70	.82	.68	.79	.72	.77	.68	—
19	.40	.77	.24	.57	.78	.58	.69	.68	.60	.51	.56	.71	.51	.58	.59	.61	.46	.77
20	.93	.68	.66	.77	.71	.88	.75	.90	.87	.89	.93	.72	.93	.82	.71	.92	.92	.71
21	.66	.94	.45	.82	.96	.76	.78	.86	.81	.78	.86	.86	.81	.76	.66	.89	.75	.80
22	.37	.57	.31	.58	.57	.48	.62	.56	.45	.56	.44	.52	.42	.53	.64	.53	.39	.67
23	.83	.55	.54	.73	.63	.86	.75	.83	.74	.77	.76	.67	.76	.79	.71	.82	.79	.67
24	.43	.67	.27	.57	.56	.43	.44	.45	.48	.43	.54	.55	.53	.44	.35	.47	.55	.38
25	.46	.48	.47	.58	.56	.59	.61	.54	.45	.45	.52	.68	.46	.66	.54	.61	.50	.48
26	.57	.56	.24	.56	.60	.56	.49	.49	.65	.59	.53	.65	.65	.59	.51	.59	.64	.59
27	.28	.49	.14	.40	.53	.40	.44	.51	.37	.29	.41	.44	.28	.43	.29	.46	.27	.43
28	.75	.62	.46	.64	.57	.68	.53	.68	.76	.70	.73	.60	.83	.60	.48	.72	.83	.53
29	.91	.50	.71	.72	.56	.86	.73	.84	.79	.82	.79	.65	.84	.60	.73	.84	.84	.60
30	.55	.68	.35	.59	.65	.60	.53	.57	.66	.53	.64	.73	.62	.59	.40	.60	.66	.54
31	.52	.55	.32	.54	.57	.52	.45	.45	.50	.53	.53	.62	.62	.64	.47	.57	.66	.58
32	.28	.48	.45	.51	.53	.39	.64	.46	.40	.45	.34	.59	.38	.50	.62	.46	.32	.61
33	.82	.57	.54	.79	.63	.83	.79	.77	.74	.86	.73	.74	.80	.81	.80	.83	.80	.68
34	.34	.49	.57	.54	.56	.44	.60	.57	.44	.50	.41	.58	.44	.56	.67	.55	.34	.57

Appendix 2: *(Cont.)*

Categories	01	02	03	04	05	06	07	08	09	10	11	12	13	14	15	16	17	18
35	.65	.52	.48	.63	.59	.71	.67	.72	.55	.58	.65	.60	.61	.73	.59	.71	.62	.54
36	.42	.63	.29	.56	.60	.47	.47	.45	.55	.41	.52	.66	.51	.47	.35	.47	.53	.43
37	.37	.39	.40	.47	.47	.50	.53	.45	.39	.38	.43	.62	.39	.57	.44	.52	.43	.44
38	.25	.32	.14	.28	.34	.29	.27	.29	.33	.21	.22	.35	.34	.31	.35	.32	.29	.30
39	.21	.46	.16	.43	.49	.33	.56	.34	.34	.43	.29	.50	.30	.37	.46	.38	.26	.56
40	.66	.65	.61	.71	.74	.74	.68	.79	.64	.63	.77	.73	.63	.81	.62	.77	.65	.60

	19	20	21	22	23	24	25	26	27	28	29	30	31	32	33	34	35	36
20	.45	—																
21	.77	.76	—															
22	.67	.42	.59	—														
23	.40	.80	.61	.39	—													
24	.34	.45	.57	.29	.32	—												
25	.44	.47	.53	.29	.56	.28	—											
26	.47	.52	.59	.32	.42	.36	.28	—										
27	.40	.32	.52	.28	.54	.13	.43	.05	—									
28	.33	.76	.63	.24	.62	.43	.27	.60	.20	—								
29	.35	.86	.58	.33	.92	.34	.57	.41	.43	.69	—							
30	.45	.59	.65	.21	.45	.79	.54	.14	.56	.49	—							
31	.31	.55	.56	.22	.44	.48	.30	.72	.03	.60	.41	.59	—					
32	.73	.30	.54	.70	.29	.24	.44	.45	.20	.20	.30	.30	.28	—				
33	.42	.77	.64	.44	.77	.31	.51	.50	.36	.61	.81	.43	.49	.36	—			
34	.73	.38	.60	.64	.38	.18	.43	.42	.36	.24	.42	.24	.27	.86	.42	—		
35	.34	.66	.55	.29	.88	.27	.64	.24	.73	.44	.80	.38	.31	.23	.60	.35	—	
36	.44	.42	.57	.20	.27	.77	.41	.42	.06	.43	.32	.90	.44	.39	.34	.25	.20	—
37	.38	.41	.45	.18	.47	.25	.97	.25	.34	.25	.49	.55	.32	.36	.45	.33	.54	.40
38	.47	.21	.35	.06	.14	.09	.15	.50	.02	.24	.20	.19	.33	.30	.19	.45	.11	.14
39	.62	.23	.47	.65	.19	.24	.28	.46	.06	.11	.14	.29	.24	.80	.37	.54	.07	.39
40	.47	.69	.71	.42	.77	.44	.77	.27	.64	.44	.73	.56	.40	.38	.57	.51	.85	.41

	37	38	39	40
38	.14	—		
39	.22	.02	—	
40	.67	.10	.17	—

Author Index

Subject Index